THEIR LIVES BEFORE US

Dagmar Strauss Yaari

THEIR LIVES BEFORE US

Dagmar Strauss Yaari

SAMUEL WACHTMAN'S SONS

DEKEL PUBLISHING HOUSE

THEIR LIVES BEFORE US

Dagmar Strauss Yaari
Copyright © 2017

Dekel Publishing House
www.dekelpublishing.com

North American rights by
Samuel Wachtman's Sons, Inc.
ISBN 978-1-941905-14-2

Editor:	Zvi Morik
Cover design:	Prof. Shimon Sandhaus
Proofreading:	Pnina Ophir

Design and typesetting by

For information contact:

Dekel Publishing House	**Samuel Wachtman's Sons, Inc.**
P.O. Box 6430, Tel Aviv	2460 Garden Road, Suite C
6106301, ISRAEL	Monterey, CA 93940, U.S.A.
Tel: +972 3506-3235	Tel: 831 649-0669
Fax: +972 3506-7332	Fax: 831 649-8007
Email: info@dekelpublishing.com	Email: samuelwachtman@gmail.com

To my sister

Noemi

With love

Acknowledgments

This book has been a long time coming, and the help I received from many corners was acknowledged in my memoir, "A Late Journey." Even so they deserve further mention.

Yaacov Lozowick, Chief Archivist, Israel State Archives, Frank Drauschke and Matthias Barelkowski from the German research group, Facts and Files, Dr. Barbara Distel, Director of the Dachau Concentration Camp Memorial Museum, Michael Viebig, Curator of the permanent exhibition, Halle Memorial, researchers Katja Seybold (Halle), Shaul Ferrero, Nadia Kahn and Yaacov Borut. Elizabeth Moatti and Elisheva Bar Shalem were most helpful with German translations.

Robbie Anna Hare, my dear friend (and literary agent) has been improving my work since 2000. I am grateful for the time she has always made available to me. Robbie, you have the sharpest eye on the planet and I'm fortunate to be one of its beneficiaries.

Thanks to Uschi Becher who translated my parents' letters in her spare time. And also to Ruth Morris who is responsible for the professional translations of the letters that appear in this book.

My beloved sister, Noemi Dalidakis, knows the depth of my gratitude for her amazing recollections of Shanghai and many other events in our family I was too young to remember. She lived my parents' lives alongside me and despite our four-year difference in age we have remarkably similar memories of our parents.

A very special thank you to Maria Sandhaus Rapoport and Prof. Shimon Sandhaus for the superb cover design that sensitively captures the essence of the story and era in which it took place.

I owe the publication of Their Lives Before Us to my husband, Ehud, who persuaded me to turn the manuscript into a book. Without his unfailing encouragement and generosity it would not have happened.

Dagmar Strauss Yaari
Jerusalem 2017

INTRODUCTION

When I first began work on this manuscript in 2001, in Israel, where I'd been living since 1992, I had no inkling that it would lead me, first and foremost, into writing my memoir. The original book, intended for my family, was to tell the story that emerged from one hundred and sixty letters my German Jewish parents exchanged in Nazi Germany between 1935 and 1939. Throughout that period, my father, Gottfried Strauss, was a prisoner of the Nazis and wrote from jail when he could, and my mother, Irene Meyer, newly married to him, corresponded from her parents' home where she went to live after my father was arrested.

How and when their letters were discovered is related in the memoir, "A Late Journey," a personal and oft times revealing account of my own life in which my parents' experiences play only a minor role. The focus of this book, however, is on them and my paternal grandfather, Karl Strauss.

The original book took close to eight years to write. Despite my commitment, the demands of travel for pleasure (mostly my husband's who is determined to see as much of the world as possible) and the necessity of many trips from Israel to Australia in order to help my sister, Noemi, in the care of our mother, made constant inroads into my writing schedule.

When the work seemed complete, a friend who'd been reading throughout suggested I show the manuscript to an American editor. Seth Schulman responded quickly and positively. He was taken with my parents' story albeit with reservations. "What's missing, though, is more of you."

Writing a book about my life had only ever occurred to me as a passing fantasy; it wasn't anything I believed I was capable of or would ever do. But Seth's observation had an extraordinarily powerful effect. It gave me permission to reexamine traumatic events in my own life that I'd played down, even ignored, in favor of writing about my parents. With Seth's encouragement I decided to write my memoir.

The change of direction created understandable dismay in my family. Explanations and justifications seemed unconvincing while I was gripped by a newfound desire to place my own life under a microscope. I hoped that I could, once and for all, arrive at a deeper understanding of myself, my choices—my life. It would be no exaggeration to claim that the task consumed me. I began to write.

It took three years to complete "A Late Journey," and a further two to publish it. Afterwards, a mental fatigue took hold and for almost eighteen months I wrote nothing. I also stopped thinking about my book. What I did instead: I set out on a frenzied spring cleaning of our apartment, throwing out pots, pans, dishes, cutlery, cooking implements, trinkets, clothes, shoes, papers, articles, cards, objects I no longer needed or hadn't even seen on shelves or at the backs of cupboards and drawers in decades. The dumping of things that had taken up too much space in our house became a metaphor for the way some of my more painful life experiences had taken up too much space in my mind. It felt good.

Then, one morning late in 2015, as I lay in bed daydreaming, my thoughts drifted towards my parents' story and the promise I had made to my family to put it into words. It began to dawn on me that I faced a familial obligation that I felt ready to fulfill, one I had set aside five years earlier. I resolved to return to my parents' letters to tell their story and that of my paternal grandfather who, together with my mother, supported my father during his years of incarceration. As the narrator, I would give myself permission to make occasional remarks when and where I saw fit.

In relating their stories I have incorporated certain chapters from "A Late Journey," and included large sections of my parents' letters to give the reader a sense of these two innocent, youthful newlyweds who clung to one another in writing throughout three long years of separation after their happiness was abruptly – and unjustly – stolen from them.

The research conducted in Germany places my parents' story in its historical context. It also provides answers to the many questions raised by their revelations to one another, and in rereading their letters, to me.

The inclusion of court reports, interrogations and statements of the judged and those who did the judging reflects an authentic picture of a thoroughly corrupt system of justice masquerading as something other than that. In a real sense, my parents' letters provide further evidence, if more is needed, of a shamefully dark period in German history.

The other major difference between this book and "A Late Journey" is that this includes photographs of the relatives I have written about. Some of these, taken in Germany in the 1930s, are precious, not only because they survived the journey from Germany via Shanghai to Australia, but because future family members will be able to put faces to relatives they might only have heard about. Other photographs are documents, evidence of suffering that Jews experienced at the hands of the Nazis.

The original letters in German, together with a body of research from the German Federal Archives in Berlin, and other institutions in Germany that collected material on my grandfather, have been promised to Yad Vashem, Jerusalem's Holocaust Memorial Museum. A copy of the originals will also be made available to the Jewish Museum in Melbourne, Australia where my parents settled after WWII and where my sister and I grew up.

A Kindle version of "A Late Journey" is available from Amazon.com. There is a hard copy at Yad Vashem in Jerusalem, the United States Holocaust Memorial Museum in Washington and the Australian Jewish Historical Society in Melbourne.

My father, Gottfried Strauss, was born in Kulmbach, Bavaria in 1907, the only child of Karl Strauss and Frieda Hamburger. Karl Strauss and his brother, Sigmund, worked in their father's business as cattle traders. Their official letterhead of 1927, which my sister Noemi Dalidakis found amongst my mother's letters, reads "Pferde und Viehhandlung" (Horses and Cattle Trading). It is not clear whether the business was established because Jews in Germany were excluded from other professions, but Karl Strauss seems always to have been struggling to make a decent living. By the late 1930's Jews were also squeezed out of the cattle trade–as they were eventually from every other enterprise–and Karl's files, found in the State Archives of Bamberg and Coburg, amongst others, show in his meticulously kept accounts that he was in dire financial straits by 1935.

Not much is known about my father's earliest childhood, although three school reports describe his academic ability and general behavior from the age of eleven.

Oddly, he displayed more talent for French and English than he did for his native German. He was good at Chemistry and Biology but poor at Commerce–an irony since he later became a successful businessman. In Physical Education he was ranked as "outstanding" which surprised me because his physique and bearing (as I noticed in my early teens) did not give the impression of athleticism. However, he was a high-jump champion at school and even at fifty-eight Noemi once saw him stand on his head to demonstrate some of his former athletic prowess. He must have had a bit of the showman in him and not only because of his mid-life hand-stands, because he once told me he learned to master conjuring tricks in his youth which he loved to perform whenever he had an audience.

At school his behavior and approach to his studies were noted as "commendable" indicating that even as a young boy he had been diligent and polite.

However, it appears from a postcard written in August 1923 by his very ill mother (three days before she died), that her son, about sixteen at the time, had a tendency to be forgetful and careless in personal matters.

"You forgot to send your shoes; your carelessness has not improved."

My father was sent to boarding school because his mother, bedridden with consumption, could not always care for him. The move away from family and familiar surroundings proved a miserable experience. He suffered cold, hunger and a constant homesickness which he kept to himself because he understood the family predicament. He waited all term for the moment he could return home for the holidays, not only to see his mother and father, but also to spend some time with his favorite aunt Hilde who often came to care for her ailing sister. Once back at boarding school, lonely and deprived of the warmth and comfort of home, my father pined for his beloved mother. When she died, after a long and painful struggle with the disease, her death affected him deeply. At age thirty, in a letter he wrote to my mother included in this manuscript, he would still refer to his mother's passing as the first truly catastrophic event in his life.

After completing his High School Intermediate Certificate, my father began an apprenticeship as a trainee buyer with a large chain of department stores in Frankfurt, far away from his hometown. It was in the firm's textile department that he accumulated a wealth of knowledge about fabrics which provided the basis for a life-long profession in the rag trade. Not yet seventeen, my father served his apprenticeship during years of galloping inflation, when his modest retainer was insufficient to both buy enough food to fill his belly and pay for somewhere to live. His paternal grandfather, Joseph, helped as much as he could, but in the end his aunt Hilde came to the rescue by arranging for him to stay with (unnamed) relatives.

Once he'd completed his apprenticeship and begun to earn a decent salary, he made regular trips to the slopes of the Italian and Swiss Alps where he became an enthusiastic and competent skier. He also learned to play the violin, an instrument for which he had enormous respect and considered the hardest of all to master.

Although he was generally intense and serious, he had a reckless side. He smoked, drank and loved gambling, a habit he indulged at the weekend horse races before my mother issued an ultimatum. Noemi told me that our mother had said to my father before they were married it was either her or the horses.

Tall, dark-haired and slightly sway-shouldered, my father peered out at the world from behind thin-framed, circular spectacles that lent him a scholarly look.

Around the age of twenty-three, Gottfried fell in love with his first cousin, Bella, whom I met in New York in 1971. Bella had the most beautiful blue eyes and regular features. When I visited her again, thirty-two years later, hoping she could tell me more about my father's earlier life she was ninety-four; her eyes had lost none of their brilliance. Apart from expressing great fondness for my father, Bella could not be coaxed into remembering more. In any event, I knew from my father that their families opposed their union, fearing for the genetic health of subsequent offspring.

I have not been able to establish precisely when and where my mother and father met, but in 1933, the year that Hitler became Chancellor of Germany, Gottfried Strauss and my mother Irene Meyer, were writing each other postcards. He was twenty-six, she, twenty-two. They were members of a Jewish youth club in Mülheim in North Eastern Germany. My father had moved there at some point and it's possible they met at the club.

My mother, Irene, was born in 1911 to Johanna Strauss and Sally Meyer, whose marriage had been arranged. Johanna looked after her three children, Irene (the eldest), Eric and Heinz while Sally went to work as a plumber.

At school, Irene excelled at arithmetic, which probably helped her find a job as an accounts clerk and bookkeeper at a retail linen business as soon as she passed her Intermediate Certificate. Her work included dealing with customer enquiries which she must have done with speed and aplomb since she boasted that she knew the account numbers of over six hundred clients by heart. Her phenomenal memory–which so cruelly betrayed her later on in life–made her a valued employee. My parents' mutual involvement with fabrics and haberdashery possibly provided a talking point when they first met.

Irene came from a home where she and her two brothers looked primarily to their mother Johanna for affection and comfort. She once said that her mother and her siblings were at their happiest when Sally was not at home. His irrational outbursts, aggravated by heavy drinking, upset their domestic peace. When the children were older, Johanna no longer tried to hide the fact that their father was a philanderer.

Nevertheless, my mother may have held a grudging fondness for her father because in one of her letters to my father she wrote:

"...the two old folks are so nice and loving to each other." Or perhaps my grandfather had seen fit to mend his ways.

It was my mother's good luck that she grew up to be a very attractive young woman. Her natural beauty captivated my father; he loved her good figure, her fine features, and her fresh, smooth and dark complexion.

In addition to her good looks and slim figure, my father found himself drawn to my mother's immense vitality and her witty and sententious style of speaking. She was so fast with her quips there were times when my father thought her a fraction superficial.

Irene was raised by a strict, but devoted mother and from all accounts, despite her sharp tongue–which her mother often censored–she was mostly obedient and a great help around the house. She inherited her religiosity from Johanna, who had come from a strictly religious home where the Sabbath and all the Jewish festivals were observed. Irene loved the customs and traditions of Judaism and at times spent the entire Sabbath at her grandparents' home. It's not known whether Irene's brothers shared her love of Jewish tradition.

Irene's brothers, whom she undoubtedly dominated by dint of her natural assertiveness, seem to have included Irene in their games and wrestling matches. In any event, she became something of a tomboy, a young girl who had confidence in the strength of her body. In a letter to my father holidaying abroad before they were married, Irene teased Gottfried with mock impatience suggesting he return swiftly so that they could have a wrestling match. She cheekily assured him she'd had the corners of a room specially padded for the occasion.

This and other letters reveal a young woman exploding with energy and joie de vivre; her sheer ebullience at being with my father leaps from her pen. What commands my attention is not only her irrepressible happiness, but her willingness to express it.

"I feel as if I'm made of iron and this is such a wonderful feeling. Do you know my darling I am so happy I can hardly keep it to myself."

After a courtship that lasted about two years, my father considered proposing marriage, but not before he had consulted his father.

Aside from the many positive character traits my father possessed, he was by nature an equivocator, a man who could so easily see all sides of an issue that it took him an eternity to make up his mind, and when he finally did, he still sometimes felt that he'd made the wrong decision. He wrote to his father:

There's my relationship with Irene Meyer, of whom I'm extremely fond and who, under normal circumstances, I would marry. Irene is strong, capable, and has real character as well as being very pretty...unfortunately, I'm finding it almost impossible to decide to marry a girl without money...I am far from being able to make up my mind, because I keep weighing up the pros and cons.

If my grandfather expressed an opinion, no letter was found in the collection with his response.

My parents had conducted their courtship against a backdrop of dramatic political and social upheaval. The Jews of Germany had weathered two years of horrendous oppression and anti-Jewish legislation and their situation was deteriorating daily. Since they were constantly losing their means of existence, my father lived in fear of destitution, which might explain his hesitation to marry "a girl without money." He was not so egocentric, however, as to think he was the answer to all of Irene's dreams. He wrote:

> What father would be happy to give his daughter to a man who has no secure source of income, like me, despite the fact that I have saved around RM7000. (In today's value, US$50,000).

In addition to personal doubts about marrying my mother, it's clear that political events weighed heavily on him.

> Last night we held our youth club jamboree which was a really lively affair–a welcome distraction from these dark and somber days. I feel that here in Germany it will no longer be possible to be happy as a Jew. One day things may be different here or in Palestine, but for now the times are full of problems for all our people... everything depends on how the Jewish question is to be resolved.

Finally, on 15th June 1935 on my father's twenty-eighth birthday, Gottfried and Irene celebrated their engagement. It is interesting that none of the postcards or letters my parents wrote to one another before their marriage mention the word love–a cultural thing, perhaps. Yet, Gottfried and Irene were in love. They were very attracted to one another and became lovers before they became man and wife, a fact my mother, already in her late seventies, once admitted after I surprised myself by asking her. We were lounging in the back garden of my house on a warm and lazy Sunday afternoon long after my father had died.

"It happened after we were engaged. I thought he'd go with other women if I refused."

Though no more was said on the subject, it reminded me that my father had once told Noemi how frustrated he'd been by my mother's initial refusal to sleep with him after they were engaged.

After an almost six-month long engagement, Gottfried Strauss and Irene Meyer stood under the chupah on 1st December 1935, and exchanged their wedding vows according to Jewish law in the presence of a Rabbi and two other (unknown) witnesses. Their civil marriage had taken place a few weeks earlier but they took the date of their Jewish wedding as the official one.

Despite their lifelong silence about their wedding day–and just about everything else that happened in the following few years– they displayed a wedding photo on the dresser in their bedroom. The picture, in sepia, shows my mother in a (presumably) white, full-length, long-sleeved and high-necked gown. She is caught in profile, looking up at my father who stands to her left smiling down at her with his right arm across the back of her chair. She wears a garland of flowers to which her gathered veil is attached at the back. In the lapel of his tuxedo, which contrasts with a white shirt and white bow tie, my father sports a tiny boutonniere.

Less than a week later their lives would change forever.

On the 7th December 1935, my father was apprehended and imprisoned by the Gestapo. During what should have been some of the happiest moments in their lives together, they were separated not knowing in such uncertain times for how long. While there are no details of the actual arrest, the Gestapo had been secretly watching my parents and certain other of his relatives for some weeks previously. This fact, together with countless others, came to me with research done in the German Federal Archives.

The Nazis had been in power for two and three quarter years during which time anti-Semitic decrees and actions towards Jews had become unprecedented in German history. The atmosphere on the streets of many cities was poisonously anti-Jewish and one wonders how bad things were for my father in prison.

However, the tone of his first letter to my mother from a place called Halle betrays none of the anxiety he must have felt at suddenly losing his freedom and finding himself at the mercy of the enemy. In fact, the letter gives the impression of the arrest being a minor temporary inconvenience. My father has even been given permission for a short visit from my mother who had gone to live with her parents.

Halle, 12th December 1935

My sweetheart,

Your letter gave me extraordinary pleasure. Despite this time in custody I'm not depressed...an involuntary parting will be followed by a joyful reunion. This might, however, take a while...the official has given permission for you to make a short visit...

My father's reference to a visit confirmed that he was writing from a prison rather than a concentration camp since visits to concentration camps were unheard of in Germany, even before they became death camps. A quick check on the Internet showed that Halle was indeed a prison, though there was no clue as to what my father was doing in a Nazi jail; I hoped the letters would eventually reveal the reason.

Noemi and I had grown up with a kind of family myth. How exactly this story came together, or who in the family was responsible for us hearing it, I'm not sure. Nevertheless, we perpetuated a tale in which our parents had borrowed my father's uncle's car to go on his honeymoon to Czechoslovakia, and had been stopped at the German border by the Gestapo. Because it was known that my father's uncle had communist connections, my father was arrested and thrown into concentration camp. I had no recollection that prison had ever been mentioned.

In any case, whether it was a foolish hope of a naïve man or a purposefully misleading promise by a prison official, my mother's visit did not eventuate. Only my grandfather was allowed briefly to see his son.

The mention of my paternal grandfather aroused my curiosity and I was hoping to learn more of the man my mother and grandmother said I physically resembled. As a youngster, I was shown a photograph of him posing in WWI military uniform with several of his fellow soldiers. Unfortunately, even with the help of a magnifying glass, I couldn't see the resemblance.

When I asked my mother what had happened to him she said he died in the war and left it at that, and I asked no further questions.

Having permission to write to each other became my parents' lifeline, and they took advantage by writing often; my mother wrote weekly, and my father, according to the changing rules of the prison. He was also allowed to receive money, and parcels of fresh clothing. I discovered during a visit to Halle in 2005, that the prison had no laundry facilities for most of the time my father spent there. Thus, I took some belated comfort, not only from the fact that my mother supplied her husband with fresh clothes, but also from learning that my father was not made to wear prison uniform. My mother took on the task of doing her husband's laundry, and without the normalcy of having her man nearby, and from a distance which spanned three-quarters of the width of Germany, helped maintain her husband's orderly physical appearance and thereby his dignity.

The absence in his first letter of any mention of charges, lawyers or bail added to my certainty that my father had been arrested for the sole "crime" of being a Jew. Random arrests of Jews, communists, social democrats and other perceived opponents of the regime were by then all too common in Nazi Germany, though often they were soon let go, their arrests having served the purpose of terrorizing Jews and other anti-Nazis. It's possible my father knew this and hoped he too would shortly be released.

Since reading the letters that ultimately led me to Germany, I have learned things about the early years of my parents' married lives that astonished me and I marvel to think they were able to keep from my sister and me. On deeper reflection, I understand. Those who survived concentration camps and death camps, and even Nazi prisons, generally did not speak about their ordeals. Where would they begin? At what moment in the course of a life would they sit down with their children to relate a personal tale of unmitigated pain and anguish? And yet, the decision (perhaps unspoken) to withhold such a life-changing period of their personal history didn't fully work. Second generation survivors say it usually doesn't because children pick up clues, often not knowing what to make of them.

Furthermore, even after reading through a large body of material from the official Third Reich archives concerning my parents, I was still left wondering about many aspects of their experiences.

In fact, I had always wondered about these two figures who dominated the first twenty years or so of my life; individually, and together, there was something about them which never felt quite right. And it wasn't just that they were German Jews striving to blend into an English Australian culture. In a vague, but very real way it was obvious that something had gone dreadfully wrong for them a long time ago that had left its invisible mark.

From the beginning it is clear my mother was taking this terrible situation in stride and her dogged determination not to be undone by the wound of their unexpected separation is reflected in every letter she writes, not least in the confident handwriting that never deteriorated into a tired or defeated scrawl. Her first surviving letter to the prison radiates happiness and encouragement. The address on her letter (Mülheim) showed that she had, indeed, gone back home to live with her parents, a fact to which all her subsequent letters attest.

Mülheim 3rd January 1936

My dear good Pappi,

You have absolutely no idea how I positively glowed this morning when I received your beautiful letter. The pleasure was quite indescribable! I beg you not to fret about me. You know that worrying is not a part of my nature…I don't do a lot of thinking, which in gloomy times is a real blessing. Your little wife is strong and has nerves of steel. If only yours could be the same.

While they were courting, my mother had written that she felt she was "*made of iron*" and in the above letter she uses the word "*steel.*" Despite her self-effacing description as someone who doesn't think deeply, she communicates durable and unbreakable images of herself, reflecting the confidence she always had in her body and strength of character. She was a woman who knew right from wrong!

Of course, neither she nor my father knew how long his imprisonment would last but one thing my mother did know was that she would wait for her husband come what may.

My mother's effusiveness demonstrated an obvious ease in expressing her feelings which I'd already encountered in an earlier letter. This relatively new and surprising aspect of her lodged in my thoughts for weeks. I couldn't digest what was, for me, a side I had never known and never imagined possible in someone as taciturn as the woman who raised me. That my mother had been a tower of strength during my father's incarceration, Noemi and I had known in some imprecise way from remarks that we'd pieced together over the years, though we were short on details. Just how short we would discover.

I've been to the doctor who assures me all is fine. He simply suggests I remain calm so that no anxiety is transferred to the baby...we do want to have a healthy child, after all, and to enjoy it, don't we!

Our parents had enjoyed married life for less than a week and yet my father seemed to know that my mother was pregnant!

From research, Noemi and I were able to work out that at the time of her marriage my mother was about five months pregnant. I examined their official wedding photo and noted that my mother is seated with her bouquet masking her belly! In any event, about a week after the letter about the baby and the doctor's advice to stay calm, my mother went into hospital and subsequently had a miscarriage. She did not mention it to my father. Instead her next letter offered utter reassurance at a time when it would have been natural to want to share their loss.

12th January 1936

My beloved,

I am absolutely taking it for granted that you are fine, and I can inform you in order to set your mind completely at rest that I'm even better. You mustn't think that this is just designed to lull you into a sense of security, I only write the complete truth to you, don't I, my pet!

We had known my mother to always tell the truth, but in January 1936, when the father of their dead baby was languishing in a Nazi prison, she lied with alacrity to make certain not to add to his anguish.

I would really like to hope that you aren't worrying about anything, since everything happens the way God intends. If you trust in God, everything will turn out fine.

My mother's faith was no surprise. She was an observant Jew even if she was not unequivocally convinced later of the existence of God. Sometime in my teens I put the question to her:

"Do you really believe in God?" Shrugging her shoulders, she replied: *"I don't know."*

When my mother came out of hospital on 18th January 1936, she wrote again to my father still not telling him about the loss of their baby.

Mülheim-Ruhr, 18th January 1936

My dearest best sweetheart,

You know, don't you, how very dear you are to me and so I hope for this reason that you are doing what I have asked... When people are as young as you and I, come what may... they can overcome disappointments of any kind. Just keep your chin up and never lose heart-that's my motto...don't get worked up and bear everything patiently. Think the way I do because spring follows winter!

Now about me: I can say that I am G.s.D (Thank God) absolutely fine and have scarcely any reason to complain...I get mail every week from your dear Father, and it always makes me happy. As I can see from what he writes he is fine, thank goodness.

The relationship between my mother and my paternal grandfather about whom she told me so little, and about whom my father never, not once, told me anything, was a truly loving one. They wrote to one another every week and my mother faithfully forwarded my father's letters which he then returned to her, and sometimes she included my grandfather's in hers to my father when the mail he was allowed to receive was limited.

The next letter from my father in the collection is dated nearly six weeks from the time of my mother's last letter.

Halle, 27th February 1936

I can't tell you how happy I am – a feeling that I've never had before. What are we going to call it? I'm sure it'll be a boy...I'd also like to ask you to eat as little as possible so that the delivery won't be too difficult. I mean this in all seriousness...You know, don't you that I have a great deal of patience. Every evening I pray to the dear Lord that we'll get through all of this all right.

The letter surprises, in that my father makes no mention of the long time during which, it seems, he heard nothing from my mother. She had written three times in January but suddenly her letters stopped. He did not refer to the silence that subsequent letters eventually explain.

I also hadn't known that my father had once believed in God and that his faith extended to him fasting in prison on the Day of Atonement. The father I knew was a declared atheist who scorned religion and I had trouble recognizing him in his letters as a man who believed in the munificence of the Creator. At one point he even asked my mother to send him a prayer book. It is not known whether she did. In any event, she now addresses the matter of their baby.

Mülheim-Ruhr, 11ᵗʰ March 1936

My dearly beloved Gottfried,

Right from the beginning of my letter I must ask you to take everything that I'm going to tell you as an act of divine providence...I can no longer hide the fact that from 8-18 January I was in the Gynecological clinic, where I had a premature birth. I deliberately kept this from you until now, on the one hand in order to spare you any more mental anguish, and on the other because when such a pain is fresh, one is readily tempted to give a blow by blow account, but now, since two months have passed, it all seems like a dream...I'm terribly sorry to have to tell you this, but please my darling, don't get upset, this is what God wanted.

My mother went on to write about the effect of the miscarriage on my grandmother:

In these circumstances as you will be able to vividly imagine, there was only one thing which really worried me – my dear Mother. Your imagination cannot possibly be lively enough

*to give you a picture of what my dear Mother went through.
She has aged by years – it is quite indescribable.*

This was one of the few occasions when my mother did not spare my father suffering. Generally, their constant reassurances to one another added to my belief that each was writing, with only few exceptions, what the other needed to read. Alone in his cell, with no one to share the grief of the loss of their unborn child who had represented a beacon of light in otherwise dismal circumstances, my father's overriding concern is for his wife and his mother-in-law:

Halle, 20th March 1936

My dear, dear lass, now you're alone again, because no baby and no Gottfried means loneliness and pain...It would have been wonderful if you and Mother had had a baby who would have brought joy into your lives...I did get very emotional when I read your letter, and yet your words always make me happy. I love your letters as much as I love you...I feel so bad for dear Mother, because she writes to me that the waiting is wearing her down.

My grandmother added a few words to my mother's response.

My dear, dear Gottfried,

I'm taking your dear lines (to Irene) to heart…don't worry about us but look after your own health and well-being…Here as always, our state of health is quite good. Look after yourself.

With all my love and kisses, from your loving Mother. Also his warmest love from Father.

The sympathy my father expresses for my grandmother's difficulty in coping with the loss is very touching, as are her short messages of love and support added to the end of my mother's letters.

Her love for my father did not surprise me but his empathy for her did, because during our lives in Australia their relationship seemed asymmetrical. My grandmother was totally devoted to him, while he seemed to take her tireless contribution to our lives for granted. She went quietly about the business of helping care for his practical needs, but I can hardly recall an occasion when he addressed her personally. In 1936, clearly things had been different.

> I hope dear Mother is also managing to keep her chin up. In her case naturally she may well suffer more than the two of us because she'll feel sorry not just for me, but also for you. I do hope that all of you will help out here, above all [your] dear Father with his sense of humor and dear Heinz too.

In the same letter of 11th March in which my mother broke the news of her miscarriage, and also informed my father that the authorities had confiscated his car and impounded his assets, she inserted a sentence which completely bamboozled Noemi and me.

> *You've written, my darling, that as a human being I'm so wonderfully pure, but unfortunately I must disagree with you, because before long I'll have to own up for the attempted abortion performed on me.*

Quite apart from my own bewilderment at the mention of an abortion, I wondered how she could have been so reckless as to refer openly, in full view of the prison censor, to an act which was illegal in Germany at the time and which incriminated them both. (Der an mir vorgenommenen versuchten Eingriff.)

My imagination ran wild. Perhaps others had forced an abortion on my unwilling mother–her helplessness accentuated by my father's absence. She might have fallen victim to experiments on Jewish women of the Dr. Mengele kind. She was after all, living in a malevolent regime where violence against Jews went unpunished and justice had ceased to have any real meaning.

But why did she seem to so readily accept the loss of her baby and even believe that it was God's will?

As the letter goes on my mother explains why she wasn't able to write to my father for nearly two months. This news was shocking.

After being released from hospital, she too, ended up in prison, held in custody for two weeks in Oberhausen, not far from Mülheim, and then in protective custody for several more. My grandmother was allowed to visit several times during her detention and she says she was allowed to write to her every week but not to my father. I wondered why?

As research later explained, simple custody in Nazi Germany would have given my mother the right to confer with a lawyer upon being apprehended. Protective custody in The Third Reich, on the other hand, was a much more serious and dangerous form of custody. It was mostly carried out by the Gestapo who could arrest Jews (and others), at will, and refuse them legal representation. Worse still, they could throw detainees into concentration camps, often without informing frantic relatives. My mother was, for reasons that were not made clear at this point, mercifully, released.

In addition to my befuddlement about my mother, my father also mentioned in his 20th March letter that he was going to stand trial, though there was still no mention of the charges.

Detention while awaiting trial always takes a few
months, and six months to a year is not uncommon.
I'm thinking the hearing will probably take place
in December but then who knows? True, I have a
good clean conscience but that doesn't always
help. Just pray to the good Lord that everything
becomes bearable.

Just as I believed that an abortion had been forced on my
mother, I was also convinced my father had been set up. No
common criminal or law-breaker, I reasoned, bothers about his
"good, clean conscience." Yet, the Nazi court seemed to have
some evidence, though in reality, they did not need hard evidence
to prosecute Jews. Justice in The Third Reich was the justice of
National Socialism where the findings of the court increasingly
corresponded to the political, anti-Semitic views of the judges.

What my father initially thought might "take a while" before
he was reunited with his bride looked, at best, as though it would
stretch to at least one year. Who knew what would happen after
that?

In the same letter in which he refers to the hearing, my father
also expresses regret that he hadn't followed my mother's advice,
further blurring the picture.

If I had only always listened to you, then everything
would be different. I know that so well.

The tendency to regret an action or decision plagued my father
from the time he was a young man.

Something had happened and the upshot of his not heeding my
mother's advice about it was particularly bitter for both of them.

There is no point in mourning the past, but
everything could have been so different, better,
if only I had been more resolute.

The greatest paradox, though – and I wonder whether, later, it occurred to either of my parents – was that the regretted decision he made that cost him years in jail probably saved their lives. Who knows whether, even after Kristallnacht, the worst pogrom in Germany's history, my father would have moved quickly enough as a free man to take the family out of the country before it was too late?

I do hope that you won't have to suffer a prison
sentence because of the operation <u>attempted</u> on
you. As far as I know, it'll be a fine. Isn't there
anything certain that you are allowed to tell me?

No matter how many times the word "attempted" cropped up, I was incapable of understanding what it meant.

Expressions of love and devotion continued to augment my parents' correspondence. They never tired of declaring their feelings for one another and after all, the letters were all they had; they literally constituted their marriage. All that was left to them was to constantly reassure one another that "everything" would turn out well–whatever that meant, exactly. My mother, in particular, never faltered.

Mülheim Ruhr, 6th April 1936

*You my most beloved in the world are my morning and my
evening prayer and my best thoughts are with you all the
time, my warmest kisses and all my love…I'm sure you are
following my advice to be brave and strong and to keep your
eyes on our happy future.*

And two weeks later:

Mülheim Ruhr, 19th May 1936

And this person beloved by relatives and friends and esteemed so much, in a word I call my very own, and I'm so proud of that.

My mother's letters show that she was capable of great love, tenderness, passion and an unstinting devotion which kept my father from breaking under the pressure of imprisonment. She fed him the food of love tucked inside each envelope she sent to the jail and it kept my father emotionally satiated and buoyant.

Halle, 3rd May 1936

The more I think of you, the more meaning there is to life. Mind you, in a way you are right when you say this makes things worse. I am quite incapable of telling you how profound and enduring my love for you is.

My father's father and my maternal grandmother were the two other unmistakable presences in my parents' lives and though my grandfather lived a long way away from my mother she traveled to visit him in early April 1936 and reported back to my father. She informed him that his father was in fine health and that his trust and faith in God helped him to bear their common fate more easily and should therefore serve as an example to both of them.

I was beginning to get a feel for my grandfather, though to this point in the correspondence I had not "heard" from him in his own words. While my mother's admiration for him and his religiosity were plain, I could not get a sense of the degree to which his fatalism governed his actions behind the scenes.

In any case, the visit greatly pleased my father and he praised my mother for not writing to him about it in advance because…it would have given me a particular pang every day had I known that you were in my home town.

With my father's almost total dependence on her, my mother's love of hard work and constant activity found a worthy cause. In fact, with all that she took on during their separation she was almost run off her feet. She couldn't do enough for him. She may have let off steam to her mother and she may have been totally exhausted but she remained upbeat when writing to my father.

While it was a considerable undertaking, my mother derived comfort from taking care of my father's laundry, from washing, starching and ironing his shirts. Together with his letters they were a tangible link connecting him to her, serving no less than as a regular confirmation that he was still alive. Before the age of automatic washing machines, dryers and steam irons, the laborious routine acted as a physical bond.

I've just ironed your shirts with more love than I've ever mustered.

Prisoners at Halle who were lucky enough to have attentive relatives, depended on them for clean clothing until some time in 1938 when the prison authorities were alerted to the practice of prisoners hiding notes in their laundry parcels. In order to prevent uncensored messages leaving or entering the prison in this way, Halle tightened its security by building a laundry. However, until the laundry was complete, Halle apparently allowed parcels to be dispatched and received, despite the risk of security breaches.

In addition to carting laundry parcels to and from the post office, my mother also sent my father library books and bought him Teach Yourself language books so he could put his free time (which was never specified) to good use.

> I just can't begin to put into words what it means for me that I'm allowed to use this wasted dead time to learn English and French. At least then, this dreadful unproductive period in my life will help me to prepare for a possible future livelihood.

My father's love of the two foreign languages had begun at school and it was ironic that in prison, of all places, he had time to advance his natural talent for them. He had no idea just how helpful for his future livelihood his proficiency in English would prove and after my parents arrived in Australia, my father taught my mother. When I was young, my parents' German accented English embarrassed me. Later, I was proud of the degree to which they mastered it.

Once the routine of sending library books had been established, my mother asked my father to return her letters in the books he'd finished with and Noemi and I assumed this was how her letters survived. As it happens, it wasn't the library books that saved her letters, as I later learned from an official at the Permanent Memorial to the former prison that now exists in Halle. The official said that the date of arrival of all letters was carefully recorded before they were read and stamped by the prison censor. They were then given to the prisoner who was allowed to keep them for a few days after which they were collected and placed in a pigeon-hole assigned to him, but to which he had no access. Upon being released or moved to another place of detention, letters and personal belongings would trail the prisoner in a separate consignment. However, they could not have been collected as frequently as the official implied since my father wrote:

> Today I've read through your last ten letters all in one go; even if I'd never seen you, or only a picture of you, I'd already love you because of the way you reveal yourself in your letters...

As to the books themselves, my father had read and enjoyed, amongst several others, Victor Hugo's, "The Hunchback of Notre Dame," and twice read Tolstoy's "Anna Karenina."

An issue which runs through my parents' correspondence and takes up much of the limited writing space–especially for my father who was allowed four small sides of paper (a little bigger than the size of a standard greeting card)–is a business matter my mother took over shortly after my father's arrest. He had been in the process of purchasing the rights to patent a sign-painting device he believed was a revolutionary tool for commercial artists and painters. Unfortunately, the business became involved in a legal wrangle which was left for my mother to sort out. She dutifully dealt with lawyers, accountants, bank managers and an apparently unscrupulous litigant.

My father believed her a capable proxy and indeed, her capacity to get things done was not only astounding, but highly admirable since she didn't share my father's belief in the device. She played along with his enthusiasm at great cost to her time and nervous energy, because he asked her to. And recognizing that my father saw it as a point of reference for his future, she was careful not to destroy that hope.

When I consider that my mother was trying to do her best in extremely difficult circumstances in which she had to wait, at certain times, up to two months to get an answer to one of her urgent questions, and when I add to that the fact that she knew my father was backing a loser, I better understand some of her later impatience with him.

By early May 1936, my mother knew that my father would be brought to Mülheim for "our" hearing. I still believed that neither my mother nor my father had done anything that in a fair society would warrant their imprisonment.

The hearing in my mother's hometown was scheduled for 5th June 1936, six months after my father was arrested. My mother seemed convinced that soon after, a non-guilty verdict would enable her and my father *to resume in the best of health the six days of blissful marriage granted us.* My mother displayed an impressive ability to stay focused on expressing her love for my father, and at the same time to bravely carry their misfortune on her young shoulders.

I have so much confidence in my heart, which is why I know and am definitely counting on justice.

With the benefit of hindsight, it is interesting to note that three years into Hitler's reign as Chancellor of Germany and Göbbels' brilliantly successful anti-Semitic propaganda, my mother still believed there would be justice for Jews.

If she was ever wracked with uncertainty, she never once allowed it to show through. In any event, the promise of physical proximity exhilarated both of them. My father, overcome with joy at the prospect of seeing his young bride again, nevertheless expressed his feelings of foreboding suggesting that he knew of, or at least suspected a bad outcome.

Unfortunately, because of the time lapses between letters, and my father's indecisiveness, there had been a mix up regarding lawyers. My father thought my mother's lawyer would be able to represent them both. Then, he changed his mind, believing there to be an advantage if she hired one for him exclusively. In the interim my mother, acting on my father's first request, engaged a lawyer to defend them both.

Halle, 25th May 1936

My passionately adored little wife,

Now, our hearing is just around the corner and you can't imagine and I simply am unable to express how much I'm looking forward to this reunion. For a short while I'll be able to see again your lovely face that I thought I couldn't live without and only circumstances have taken away from me for such a long time. What enormous joy combined with melancholy. But your love my darling gives me the courage to bear the blows of fate that cannot be sidestepped. So much so that separations like ours of whatever length and distance can for us have only one consequence: the greatest possible love. This love is happier by far than any other not also born out of deep suffering.

Since there might be a chance of you, my love, also getting a prison sentence, I suggest you discuss the most important matters regarding the patent business with Heinz.

Even in extremis, my father had one eye on his current misfortune while the other one remained firmly fixed on his business interests.

The day of the reunion, when the young couple stood in an impersonal courtroom gazing at one another, was the day when the full force of what had happened to them hit my father with monumental intensity, though he did not reveal his feelings until much later.

My father knew that forced separation produced a heightened, more intense kind of loving. He seemed almost grateful for the experience.

Evidently, my parents were involved in something together, yet my father had been arrested while my mother was only questioned and released.

No sooner had I been processed than I received a letter from my dear Father which was sent on to me from Halle, and to my great joy on Saturday morning I also received your lovely lines. So, I wasn't alone here in my cell - you and all my beautiful memories are much closer to me here than in Halle...when it comes to pluck and courage you are equal to me, if not superior...Just tell your dear Mother that I regret everything from the bottom of my heart, but every individual has the supreme duty to bear the consequences of his actions with dignity. We have not given our loving families much joy, and I am aware that I am to blame, but like you I think that when it comes to things one can't change, one must resign oneself to the situation, however difficult this may be...

All my love and kisses from your

Gottfried who loves you.

The morning of 5th June 1936 remained in my father's memory a lifetime. The reunion with my mother was an epiphany in which he was faced, inescapably, with all that had been lost though he kept that to himself for close to two years. In isolated moments only, when he was overcome with the wretchedness of his lot, did his letters hint at the despair that threatened to overwhelm him.

While my parents' letters spoke chiefly of their excitement and longing, my father's happiness was mingled with "regret for everything."

Despite the solemnity of the occasion and perhaps because of it, I imagine my mother wore her smartest summer outfit, complete with matching accessories including a hat, which she once told me was a convention required of married Jewish women appearing in public, even if they were not strictly religious. She would have taken special care to comb her fine dark hair, and carefully apply her lipstick–the only make-up she ever used–as I'd seen her do so many times as a child.

I visualize my father, his eyes searching for my mother the moment he enters the chamber. They settle on her and he is enthralled by her beauty. The months in between have blurred his visual memory.

The court session flies by in what feels like seconds and neither of them knows when they will see each other again. My mother is not detained. Not only is she still a free woman, but my father can continue counting on her incomparable support.

Early on in my work I had my hopes pinned on what my parents' letters might disclose after their Mülheim hearing. I hoped that once my mother and father had appeared in court, all would be revealed. Unfortunately, it wasn't and I was left still having to infer meaning, with the help of odd references, much as I'd been doing before. The hearing came and went without one word to each other in their subsequent letters alluding to the trial or its outcome. The desire for clarity remained utterly frustrated.

Later on that same day, my mother got out her writing pad.

My dearest, most beloved darling,

Today we were granted proof that the good Lord has once again stood by us.

I assumed my mother was expressing relief and gratitude to the Almighty that she was not required to serve a term behind bars as my father had feared.

I am immensely glad to have seen you again after such a long, involuntary separation. There are undoubtedly happier reunions, but as you know, my darling...I am firmly convinced that the rain is followed by bright sunshine, and this should help you too to stay brave and strong.

My mother mentioned an illness which she assured my father was not serious. There were no more allusions to the trial.

As soon as I'm completely healthy again, I'll get a job...I would definitely not have written this if my illness was disquieting, but thank God it isn't dangerous. The only thing to be done, according to the doctor, is rest and patience.

My father replies:

Halle, 10th June 1936

My adored treasure,

You have no idea, my dearest one, how much seeing you again, even though we were not allowed to speak to each other, affected me, positively speaking. Your wonderful nature and the image of

your beauty which I love so much again inspired
me so greatly that no sacrifice could be too much
for me to bear in order that I can once again be
reunited with you. This marvelous future and hope
would enable me to bear any length of sentence
easily...I have to give you a dressing down.
How can you relate so light-heartedly to your
illness and do nothing about it...I want you to
go to a spa...You'll be able to get a loan from
relatives whom you've helped in the past. My
Father will help too...Things mustn't fall down
on this account-this thought would drive me to
despair.

My mother's mention of an illness panicked my father. He depended on her. For emotional reassurance he received her constant words of love and encouragement. If he requested mental stimulation she sent him books. His dirty clothes were returned to him freshly laundered. He read her letters until he knew them by heart. For all these reasons she needed to be well and, no less importantly, she also needed to work. Since the Nazis had confiscated my father's assets, she'd had to dig into whatever savings she had. She never gave her mystery illness a name though she does refer to it;

> *...on my right side I still have an inflammation...my left side, incidentally, has completely healed. You just can't imagine how robust my little body is. But you know, don't you, that I've always lived for my health. My blood is first rate.*

In his 10th June 1936 letter, before signing off my father asked for more information about my mother's condition but she couldn't enlighten him:

You want me to tell you what the illness is called? Well, I just can't because I myself don't know. The nice doctor rattles on in a most refined way, using Latin terminology and I don't understand a word he's saying and it doesn't bother me because I'm not in the least bit curious. I have no pain, and in the last days the temperature has gone down.

In due course my mother was treated for whatever ailed her.

...in order to avoid being nagged [by you] I've decided to take the doctor's advice to go to hospital for two weeks for proper treatment.

She was accepted into the ward like any other German, though the staff must have known she was Jewish. Apparently, she suffered no discrimination from either her fellow patients or the nursing staff; on the contrary, her youthful audacity and high spirits earned her the reputation of a leading mischief-maker.

29th June 1936

On Tuesday morning I moved here to St. Marien Hospital where I have become part of a group of people, being one of the less ill patients. I'm not exaggerating if I say that it's like being in a Punch and Judy show...It's impossible to do anything because the patients here are always kicking up a racket, and the music is blaring on the radio. The residents of this ward are no paragons [of good behavior] and that includes me too! I am known as "rascal!" The only people in our ward are those who are not in pain.

The description of my mother as a ringleader of bored and rebellious patients never failed to amuse me.

What is striking about my mother's picture of St. Marien's is the contrast between it and the world of Nazi Germany outside. She describes an atmosphere of frivolity and harmless disorder in which the patients, restless in their confinement to hospital, are trying to have as much fun as they can.

Their acceptance of her plus a mention in a previous letter that they all shared the wry sense of humor that residents of Mülheim are known for, would seem to indicate that pernicious anti-Semitism in the mid-1930s was by no means evenly spread throughout Germany.

My mother's treatment consisted of constant bed rest, four freshly filled hot water bottles a day, and *"one hour of hot air twice a day."* Whether the air was blown at her, over her or whether she had to inhale it is not specified. The major procedure, however, involved being wrapped up for six hours at a time in a Tubatherm pack–a treatment still used in Germany today–that was supposed to help treat whatever she was suffering from. It consists of warm packs applied to one or several parts of the body using materials such as mud, salt or fango which is made from ground and pulverized Kaiserstuhl volcanic rock. Every pack is prepared freshly with thermal waters and applied hot and moist to the body for long-lasting effects.

As she wrote in her 9th July letter, my mother astonished the nurses with her ability to withstand high temperatures while remaining relaxed and uncomplaining.

The only parts of my mother's body that were not included in the heat pack were her head and arms. She was thus able to continue her correspondence with my father, albeit from a horizontal position– *"I am only able to sit up when the nurses aren't looking"*–which presented some problems. She found it hard to get the ink to flow in her fountain pen so she switched to pencil, which caught the vexed attention of the Halle censor, Dr. Schwartz. Displaying a grudging streak of humanity, he scribbled a note at the top of one letter: "Inform the sender that only clear script will be passed on [to the recipient]. I'm allowing it through, only in consideration of the illness." The hot packs actually pleased my mother because she'd heard they left the patient *lovely and slim.* Only in her case, the three-week treatment, probably due to inactivity, had the opposite effect and she emerged from it a *chubby chops.*

Health was an issue in every letter. My father had begun his detention as a fit young man. However, the cruel interruption of his marriage, his loss of freedom, and the uncertain length of his confinement made him emotionally vulnerable. And my mother knew it because she knew her man. There is hardly a letter where she does not exhort him to remain strong and her meaning is unequivocal.

> *...I do hope and even expect that you, my dearest darling, will do everything that is good for your health...For if you allow your nerves to get frayed I am the one who is most affected and I'm sure you don't want that to happen.*

My mother had no qualms about demanding behavior from my father that was in her interests as well as his.

Being only in their twenties their obsession with health may seem surprising, yet its importance cannot be overstated. Mental and physical health were the imperatives for survival in circumstances of such grave adversity in which Jews found themselves and even then, did not guarantee it. A cavalier attitude to what most young people of my parents' age take for granted in normal times was not possible for them.

After his Mülheim hearing, my father wrote of his incarceration becoming routine and it seemed like a genuine claim.

Halle, 19th June 1936

The secret of this "bravery" is to be found in custody becoming a habit. I believe that the effect of punishment for anyone who hasn't yet been in jail is mainly confined to the first six months...At the moment, the days rush by in a flash. Sometimes...when I'm reading something enjoyable until dusk, I have quite often wished I had a bit more of the day to do so. I make sure my thoughts do minimum straying beyond the walls and that way I fare best.

Yesterday [June 18], I had the great joy of a visit by Father. Unfortunately, he got very worked up, while I neither shed a tear when he arrived nor when he left. Instead, I managed to calm him down and offer reassurance, since I know that all the mental anguish comes about—both in my Father's case and in yours and in your Mother's—mainly out of sympathy with my lot. I do hope that I have managed to give my little wife, whom I love beyond all else in the world, as well as my Father, sufficient evidence that in this respect I'm better off than all of you.

Normally, my mother and grandfather coordinated their prison visits not only, I presume, due to the paucity of visits permitted and the time available to each to travel the long distance. They could also support one another and use the opportunity to speak face-to-face about anything that needed to be arranged for my father.

What is touching about the 18th June visit is that father and son have reached that crossroads in a child-parent relationship where the younger is able to console the older. In my father's case, after seven months in prison, the process of de-sensitization had begun as a way of surviving, emotionally and mentally, making it easier to remain strong in the presence of his worried father.

Every mention of my paternal grandfather added to my curiosity about him.

My father continued his 19th June letter:

Although I keep examining over and over again the substance of my case, I see no grounds whatsoever which could lead to me being found guilty and so for the most part my mood is pleasant and confident.

Mülheim, 21st June 1936

I've already heard from Father that he visited you. He seemed to be over the moon...I can well imagine dear old Dad getting dreadfully upset. He's a real softie who cries easily, but then he feels better. Why shouldn't he? Everyone has his own way of behaving...I am also terribly fond of him because he's an extremely sweet, generous and good person, and especially because he's your father.

It seemed obvious that, due to censorship, my parents could not discuss the substance of my father's case. More than half a year had passed since my father's arrest and they'd not been able to speak. My grandfather had been to see my father twice. Had my father and grandfather exchanged important information during the latter's two visits which my grandfather then conveyed to my mother? Did my father's lawyer keep in touch with my mother? In approximately six weeks my father would table an official document containing a vast amount of information about his case, which found its way into my parents' private correspondence. However, it is not possible to tell when my mother received it. It is equally impossible to say what she knew at any given time.

Guided by the chronology of the letters, I saw that by 11th July 1936 my father had been brought to Duisburg (a neighboring town to Mülheim) for another trial which would detain him there for a month. There was still no description of his crime but this time my mother did not appear to be involved. My father, desperate to see her, begged her to apply for a visitor's permit.

In response she wrote:

Although I am not in favor of half measures such as seeing you from afar, I will of course happily come to Duisburg if this would please you.

The half measures my mother referred to seem to be the physical distance that had separated her from my father in the Mülheim courtroom three weeks previously. As it happened, she did visit my father in Duisburg and later let slip that my father's incarceration was more difficult for her to endure than she'd been prepared to admit since referring to *"the hard things"* was something she rarely did.

Mülheim, 5th August 1936

Now that I have had time once again to think things over, I am, after all, pleased to have seen you again, my beloved dear one. When I see your image before me, as you look at me with your dear devoted eyes, despite everything I am overjoyed. And then in my mind's eye I go forward in time

*and imagine a picture of how I will "cherish you." I'll do all
the dear, beautiful things for you then, my darling. Yes, my
angel, that is the hope that lives in me and which helps me
to more easily bear all the hard things.*

My father responded:

```
You my beloved child indulge in thinking about
how wonderfully you're going to shape the future
for me and to this extent our thoughts coincide.
Unfortunately, I think only too often of how much
more enjoyable the past could have been if we had
shaped our time more beautifully.
```

If my parents had been chatting in the kitchen of our home,
my father could not have displayed an attitude more typical of
himself and my mother a less typical one. Her capacity for real
loving, expressed to my father in honeyed sentiments that gave
him hope, afforded me a brief look into the chasm between how
she had been before and how she was afterwards. There were
many unforeseeable hardships and disappointments for both of
them yet my mother's transformation when held up against the
letters seemed more dramatic. During my life with my parents,
my mother was by and large an emotionally closed book though
in retrospect it is understandable; despite their youth, the years of
separation and gut-churning anguish simply eroded their reserves
of emotional energy and perhaps ironically, my mother's more
than my father's.

On 10th August 1936, eight months after my father's arrest, he
composed a letter to the Halle Magistrate's court at the suggestion
of the Magistrate who first remanded him into custody. This
official had advised him to prepare additions, amendments and

extra evidence to the summary of the statements he made during his questioning by the Gestapo. Why it had taken my father so long to follow the Magistrate's advice is unknown.

Though it was impossible to reconstruct a complete account of the events my father referred to, however obliquely, in his statement, it added a considerable body of information to what I had gleaned from my parents' letters. On the face of it, the court's invitation to my father to supply extra proof of his innocence, gave the impression of a just legal system. However, the appearance of the document in the collection is perplexing, since it is not addressed to my mother yet came into her possession, complete with the censor's stamp.

In any event, three new players entered the story; my father's uncle and aunt, Dr. Gustav and Hilde Flörsheim, and their friend Franz Krause. The following is an abridged version of my father's letter.

10th August '36

To the
Magistrate's Court, Division 12
Halle

At the time of my interrogations by the Hallo Stapo, I believed that I was being questioned as an uninvolved witness, and not as a joint indictee. However, it appears this is not so.

As far as I can remember, in the statement [taken from my questioning] it says: "I knew that Krause was operating illegally against Germany and was making common cause with Gustav Flörsheim." The way in which this is stated goes beyond any information I actually had. At a brief meeting at my relative's home in 1934, I remembered Krause as an

inveterate moaner who fiercely criticized the government's measures and was supported in his views by Flörsheim. A year later my aunt and uncle [Flörsheim] told me that Krause had emigrated to the C.S.R because of his [anti-Nazi] views, though I failed to discern either the scope or the nature of his activities in Germany and later in the C.S.R; this only became clear to me after my involuntary trip with my uncle Flörsheim to Tetschen. If my uncle had told me the plain truth before the journey to Tetschen, then my accompanying him there could never have taken place. However, I was in the dark about Krause's operations and the real relationship between him and my uncle.

I also wish to deny that there was any talk of spying.

Lastly, my request to Krause to help me with my patent business in Russia was free of political motives.

There was, after all, a history to my father's arrest and imprisonment. It was no longer possible to believe that he'd been arrested simply because he was a Jew (although his Jewishness undoubtedly made matters worse). His association with his uncle Gustav and his uncle's friend, Franz Krause, whose political views were antithetical to The Third Reich, lay at the heart of his detention. Krause had obviously slipped through the Gestapo's hands and fled to Tetschen, Czechoslovakia, where Flörsheim, together with my father, went to visit him. This information about my father was distressing since I knew he was never politically active (though he was happy to discuss politics) and indeed, it transpired that he went to Tetschen against his will.

My father went on to describe how it had taken his uncle–a medical doctor–three days to wear him down, before he finally agreed to the trip. It appeared that Flörsheim was not averse to using emotional bribery to get his way, arguing that my father was in his debt for free medical assistance and extended hospitality. My father's aunt also pressured my father, because she wanted her nephew to try and convince Krause to break off his relationship with her husband. My mother did not rate a mention in this document.

Nazi Germany was a terror state which brooked no political opposition, and in which, therefore, it was dangerous, even in private, to mix with those, including family, who "fiercely criticized the government's measures," since informers operated everywhere.

My father's statement to the Halle Magistrate showed there were points at which the family myth Noemi and I had grown up with converged briefly with reality–my father had indeed gone to Czechoslovakia (albeit without my mother), but there were significant differences and omissions.

Along with my belief that my father had been thrown into prison because he was Jewish, went a blindness about what might have happened to him there. I hadn't considered that he'd undergone interrogation by the Gestapo, probably because it was a thought too awful to contemplate. When he actually referred to his questioning, I shuddered, because I knew from my research that in certain instances, physical force had been used on political prisoners in Halle to extract confessions. When I first came across his letter to the Halle magistrate I didn't know whether my father belonged in this category of prisoners, yet the mere possibility sickened me.

A whole world existed behind the scenes of my parents' correspondence about which I had been totally unaware.

Questions arose that my father's statement didn't address. Why had he initially resisted his uncle's request to go to Czechoslovakia if, as he says, he was unaware until after the trip of the full scope of Krause's anti-Nazi activities and the true nature of his relationship with his uncle? And why did my father feel he needed to explain that his request to Krause for business advice had no political overtones? Also, what kind of free medical assistance and extended hospitality did my father's uncle provide?

My father's capitulation to his aunt's entreaties I could understand. She had, after all, nursed his dying mother (her sister). My father was a tender-hearted man who could be manipulated and who often found himself roped into other people's problems. And besides, if it were true that my father had enjoyed the Flörsheims' hospitality, he would have felt obliged to return that kindness. That it took him three days to arrive at the wrong decision was sadly predictable. Was this his meaning when he wrote shortly before his Mülheim trial in June 1936 that he regretted not standing his ground?

Some time in early August 1936 my mother was well enough to go for a job interview in Essen, a neighboring city to Mülheim. The position on offer, Store Manager of a (Jewish) apron factory, appealed to her. However, despite liking the man who interviewed her, she turned the job down because they couldn't agree on a number of (unstated) conditions. She was not in the least discouraged claiming, *"there are enough jobs and so I'm not in a hurry."*

This claim seemed puzzling since random dismissals of Jews and takeovers of Jewish enterprises became more common as the Nazi era progressed.

In any event, some days after her interview, a phone call persuaded my mother to change her mind, since the fellow who'd interviewed her had apparently changed his. He would meet her demands and wanted her to begin work immediately. She was flattered by his eagerness to employ her since apparently there'd been many applicants. She was to be given a trial period of four weeks, and in her self-effacing way announced:

If I'm not too stupid, they'll probably keep me on.

Predictably, my father's reaction was mixed:

Halle, 23rd August 1936

I was particularly surprised and delighted by your news of being taken on in Essen...nevertheless, I am sorry that fate has not dealt more kindly with you and that you have been forced to go back into the workforce.

My father had intended to support his young bride. She would stay home and keep a perfectly run house and wait for babies to arrive. She would spend her free time knitting, crocheting and sewing beautiful clothes for them. Family members would come to dinner on Friday evenings to welcome in the Sabbath or they would go to my grandparents' place and on Saturday, husband and wife would go to the synagogue, while my grandmother baby-sat. On Saturday afternoon the house would be open to guests for "Kaffee und Kuchen." In the bigger picture, the Germans would soon wake up and object to their Nazi rulers; they would become increasingly ashamed of their leader's treatment of their fellow citizens, the Jews, and eventually overthrow him, ridding the country of this unparalleled period of anti-Semitism.

It was a pipedream.

From the time she realized that my father would not be released within days or even weeks of his arrest, my mother knew she'd eventually need to find work. My father understood it too, and in addition to all the other blows his ego had sustained, being supported by his wife was another one.

My dear child, I know that you have a very good (nature) in this respect, but you won't be accustomed any more to working in a business.

What may appear at first to be the words of a considerate man, were in truth the projections of one who doubted himself, and by extension, also doubted others. Though he intended no offence his words were somewhat patronizing. Happily, it didn't bother my mother:

You're happy that I have a job, but on the other hand you're again sorry that I'm working. How can this be reconciled? You sweet man, don't torment yourself with pointless thoughts.

Though it's not mentioned directly, I'm certain that from the moment my mother got herself a full-time job, she began saving for the day my father would be released. While she didn't yet know when that would be, she was practical and mature enough to understand that whatever happened, they would need money and, in any event, regularly putting aside a discreet sum to build up one's nest egg was an accepted imperative of my parents' upbringing. It was the way people like them—who were not born into wealth—got on in the world.

Nine months had passed in which my mother may have had to accept handouts from relatives to supplement whatever money she'd saved from previous jobs, although I find it difficult to imagine my mother doing that since she was fiercely proud. In any event, after taking the job in Essen, she could begin to work towards more financial independence, a status which made her feel good. She could also, with an easier mind, send my father 10RM a month, which he'd requested in order to buy himself newspapers and cigarettes.

Their correspondence during the month of August 1936 featured reports about my mother's job, the regular enquiries and assurances about each other's health and expressions of love and devotion. My grandfather had invited my mother to visit him in Kulmbach but she'd written that first she needed to complete her series of treatments before she could contemplate travel. Although she'd finished at the hospital at the end of July, she still needed regular check-ups that would keep her in Mülheim. She began her job on the 15th August and I can't imagine she'd have asked for time off so soon.

On the 18th August my mother had changed her strategy of not mentioning matters to my father that would add to his longing. Now, she drew his attention to his late mother's "Jahrzeit," the annual Jewish commemoration of a loved one; she'd previously glossed over family events she knew would sadden him but this time made a point of reminding him ahead of time to say the memorial prayer for his late mother, adding that she would light the traditional candle in his stead. My father expressed his gratitude:

...because of your reminder I observed my Mother's Jahrzeit.

At other times, my father was glad to be told of happy family celebrations after they'd taken place as on the occasion of his brother-in-law Eric's wedding:

For Eric's wedding, I send belated congratulations. It was very tactful of you, my good little one, to first hint at it and only then tell me when it had happened. By doing it this way, you spared me a great deal of mental anguish, you sweetie.

Two paragraphs in my father's letter of 23rd August 1936 particularly piqued my interest.

I'm still in pre-trial detention and I don't yet know when I'll be moved to penal confinement. Both are bearable, and I just wish that the main hearing were soon. I don't think it will be before the end of the year.

And,

Real life is only just beginning for the two of us, and it really would be the best thing if while I'm in jail one could deliberately and cruelly turn off memory and reciprocal pity and put oneself in a state of indifference, as you, my beloved dear soul, have shown me.

My father's words seemed to indicate that he was found guilty of something in Mülheim and Duisburg and because of it would be moved from the court prison where he'd been held on arrest up until now. The phrase, "real life is only just beginning" would become clear in time.

In my mother's reply she stuck to subjects she felt comfortable with, feeding him a diet of the minutiae of her everyday life, including her new job. She judged this approach to be a useful distraction.

Mülheim, 30th August 1936

It's now a fortnight since I started my job…It's just as well I have a fairly thick skin because otherwise I mightn't be there anymore. I wouldn't be exaggerating if I were to tell you that on Friday nothing my pen wrote was right. I let all the carping go by without reacting for a long, long time, until evening, and then the bomb exploded. You can well imagine, my dearest dear, can't you, how Tutti cursed and swore. [He's] a proper monster! In the evening when he comes into the office from his daily rounds, that's when the children's entertainment hour begins. His sister, the office boss and <u>person in charge</u> rolled into one, a "charming" creature of around 45, a redhead, then has to take dictation and carry out instructions. "Miss Strauss" is called in as inspector. You can well imagine that I don't just stand there during such a performance–every so often I erupt.

What I really <u>like</u> is that things are checked five times. On Friday, after our heated discussion, he tried to apologize on the grounds that he's very on edge. Yesterday he was charming again, which goes to show that what I said did some good. He can't use his moods, which govern him, against me.

"He" has noticed that he's not dealing with some spineless creature. That'll do for now…

During the day I don't have time to think of you, my beloved sweetheart, but if you could only hear how I talk to you in my dreams at night and all the encouragement I call out to you, I'm sure you'd definitely comply with my wishes…I bid farewell to my dearly beloved Gottfried with "chazak". i.e. [The Hebrew word for "strong."]

Later that year, my mother continued to offer my father some light relief with more tales of the boss's sister:

For a few days I've been having a running battle with "her," the ugly cow. I've told her she shouldn't even dare to speak to me for the time being. When the bee is being mean she will sting! See how pugnacious I am, my darling. It's a funny old world, innit! Quite ridiculous, straight out of the pages of Punch. When she thinks there is no one looking [she places] one finger in her mouth and one on her head…Now there's a picture for a magazine. "He" also has very amusing habits. When he gets stuck while dictating, he chews his handkerchief. Charming, isn't it? Sometimes it strikes me that I've landed in a freak show or the waxworks!

In this way my mother kept my father grounded, through his long and lonely ordeal, by bringing day-to-day life into his detention and by demonstrating to him in a humorous way that the woman on whom he was relying was nobody's fool. Since my father seemed to thrive on the details of my mother's employment, she obliged him with yet more stories.

…I have to keep a large number of books. Store books, returns books, incoming goods, outgoing goods, cash book, order book and many others I'm not yet familiar with. Check goods which come in, make goods available for making up in the sewing room, keep three sets of books about that.

Make cutting slips, transfer to cutting book, then change again, sort finished goods by sizes and items, again enter in three sets of books, until everything is in the storeroom in a well-ordered fashion. Deal with home workers (a horrible, protracted business), serve store's customers and the main thing, shipments to firms...there's plenty of work for three people–that's the minimum, I can tell you, but the good fellow [the boss] is a pretty jittery creature!

My father believed that the amount of work was "incredible" and was only mildly concerned about her boss's treatment of her because he knew "that Tutti makes sure that she gives as good as she gets."

My mother's boss is never given a name, and it's impossible to know whether the man was neurotic by nature, or was reacting to a steadily worsening economic situation for Jews. After all, the Nazis were closing down Jewish businesses and forcing sales of Jewish enterprises, reasons enough to make him a nervous wreck.

Despite the huge amount of work, the time it took her to travel and my mother's other commitments, she found time in her life and in her heart for my grandfather, not only in the weekly letters she wrote him but in other ways:

This week I'll send him some material for a pair of trousers.

About five weeks after my father's 10th August statement to the Halle magistrate, he was moved from the court prison of Halle into penal confinement to begin serving a six-month sentence.

My mother expressed surprise when a good part of the fresh laundry she'd sent him arrived back at her home. My father's watch and wedding ring were returned too in the same package. During the Nazi era, personal items such as these were sometimes returned to the relatives of Jews who had "suddenly and mysteriously disappeared."

From penal confinement my father raised a new subject:

Halle, 13th September 1936

The outcome of my trial is after all completely uncertain...it is an especially unenviable fate in this period to be under the suspicion that has attached itself to me.

But what began as a depressing letter quickly turned into one offering some reason for hope.

As a result I am firmly convinced that for me and hence for us, it would be an important advantage if, by my hearing, I were in possession of an affidavit from the USA and the papers and documents needed for emigration. My lawyer shares my opinion. Even though I am not aware of having done any wrong, nevertheless I cannot tell you, my dearest little one, in as much detail as I would like, in how many respects it could be helpful for my subsequent liberty if I could provide proof that on the basis of connections, I could move my domicile abroad, i.e., to the USA. Please, my darling, do me the favor of moving heaven and earth, trying every possible channel needed in order to attain this goal.

A week later my father wrote again, but from this date on his permission to write would be restricted:

Halle, 20th September 1936

I've been in penal confinement (Strafthaft) since Thursday and I'm pleased that I've been allowed to begin serving my six month sentence now; what has been got out of the way will be behind me. My sentence runs from 18.9.36 to 18.3.37. In the meanwhile, at least I hope so, there will probably be my [main] hearing and we'll have to take whatever else gets handed down. Unfortunately, I'm now only allowed to write to you once a month, but I can receive mail as frequently as up to now...this and other privileges up to date will now be discontinued...I now no longer need money since I won't be able to buy anything, and so I can't give my sweetheart the pleasure of looking after me in this respect.

My mother would have understood the reason for the returned laundry; my father was now wearing prison uniform.

My grandfather enquired soon afterward, whether he could send his son a warm blanket. Apparently not:

The dear fellow! Of course this is quite out of the question.

In the same letter my father continued:

My dearest, you talk of me having the right thoughts at a given moment...I would advise you too to try very hard to remember all possible details of our last stay as well as what you stated when you were in protective custody, so that one day you too will be able to have the right thoughts.

Constrained by censorship, my father nevertheless tried to convey to my mother the critical importance of their stories matching, which indicated that he knew she had been interrogated. It should have been obvious to me also, but when I first read their letters it wasn't. However, their inability to coordinate their version of events with such restricted communication–due largely to censorship and the limited number of letters my father was now allowed to write–would, in the end, prove damaging.

A week later my mother referred to the "right thoughts" at any given moment.

> *I cannot now say in what context I wrote this, perhaps I didn't express myself quite clearly, but you didn't understand me properly. However, I will give my intense consideration to all the details of our stay in Zeitz. Things which I don't enjoy remembering I always manage to file away in a flash...I don't remember a single word of what I said when I was in protective custody. But not to worry, it'll come, my beloved sweetheart! All with God's help!*

Lapses in time and censorship had contributed to confusion and misunderstandings. Additionally, my grandfather was often slow in returning my father's letters which my mother sent on to him, so that sometimes she answered my father from memory. In one letter she writes:

> *Both letters (my father's to her and to his father) are visiting Kulmbach, which is why today I can't go into your lovely letter in as much detail as I would like to. But I'll make an effort and tax my brain.*

Of interest was my mother's description of how she dealt with unpleasant matters. Her knack for filing away the hard things–in a later letter she also claimed that she'd dispensed with sentimentality–enabled her to respond to my father's problems with a cool head. She claimed it was one of her greatest strengths and also that it was God-given. Later on, however, the "filed away things" may have contributed to her frenetic approach to living, her tendency to fill every minute of the waking day with yet another activity.

In his 20th September letter, my father was able to add clarity to his urgent request. When I first read my parents' letter I did not truly comprehend the terrifying implications of my father's explanation.

Halle, 20th September 1936

I repeat this [acquiring affidavits] is the only chance which might perhaps help prevent me, if I am acquitted, from going back into preventive custody. I'm absolutely convinced that it would influence the court's decision if I were to present proof that I had the opportunity to make a new life for myself outside the country. Would you, my darling, throw all your energy into this?

Here was a stunning example of so-called Nazi justice. In Germany, in late 1936, a served sentence did not guarantee freedom for a Jew.

The initiative my father had failed to take in 1934 when emigration to Palestine had been on his mind, had suddenly grown into an imperative. My parents' youthful fantasies of taking up normal married life exactly where they'd left off, before my father's arrest, vanished.

In her typically unflustered and efficacious manner, my mother flew into action. She did even more than was being asked of her. In her next letter she reported that she'd written letters to my father's cousins in the USA, and to an aunt of hers in South America. She'd made contact with the Palestine Office in Berlin, and was planning to go there personally to see if in that way she could hasten the acquisition of entry permits. She registered with the Central Office for Jewish Emigration Relief and The Aid Society for Jews in Germany, two organizations which were working hand-in-hand to deal with the worsening situation of Jews. She also reported on my grandfather's efforts:

Dear Father wrote to me yesterday, as follows: We've all written to America already, I'm absolutely convinced that everybody over there will vouch for us.

My grandfather's use of the word "us" indicated that he intended leaving Germany with his son and daughter-in-law if and when visas finally arrived. My mother assured my father:

As you wish, I'm throwing all my energy into this.

She had not given up on "the good Lord," who she was sure was *"bound to help,"* but she clearly wasn't leaving all urgent matters up to Him.

Responding to a letter of my mother's in which she had made the point several times that she was undaunted and unaffected by other people's happiness, including her own brother's wedding, my father felt moved to applaud her.

```
You are such a practical philosopher of life.
What other great thinkers put into words, you
simply put into practice...you're unproblematic,
straightforward, and a model for how to live.
```

Do you remember, my beloved Irene, how I once
considered your approach to be unpleasant? Oh,
how greatly have I changed my views and my rules
for life.

And my mother said of herself:

*I've changed a great deal…I've become far, far more mature
– I'm no longer the Tutti who always looked for excuses in
serious and important matters in order not to have to deal
with them. I used to be easy-going and superficial, now I
prefer to work out difficult and more profound matters.*

Small wonder that my mother's personality was undergoing
changes as she rose to meet what was probably the toughest test
of her life. It is hardly an exaggeration to say she was carrying my
father's life on her shoulders, and in spite of her profound devotion
and unfailing encouragement, she seems to be conveying, to herself
as much as to my father, that the ordeal of his imprisonment and
the events surrounding it could not possibly leave her the same
person as she was before.

My mother revealed another side to her personality with her
penchant for poetry. Several times throughout the correspondence
when, perhaps, she thought others encapsulated thoughts better in
verse than she could express, she would copy it:

"Have sun in your heart
whether it's storming or snowing
whether the sky is full of clouds
the earth is full of strife
have sun in your heart
(Cäsar Flaischlen)
And on another occasion:

Night is not forever
Nor winter's want
And there is no everlasting pain!
After every storm the sun shines brightly
The power of life conquers death
And every heart forgets the time
that once gave it grief
(**GERTRUDE BIELER**)

The poetry sprinkled throughout her letters underscored the fact that my mother had indeed changed and that she kept so much of what she'd once been in a very private part of herself.

As the legal battle in my father's patent business intensified, complicated by his absence and my mother's unfamiliarity with basic commercial law, she reported that she was less and less able to keep on top of *the real mess* though not for want of trying. The more lawyers and litigants who entered the fray, the more muddled things became and my mother was barely keeping her head above water. She had a full-time job to which she commuted between Mülheim and Essen six days a week. (Despite being a Jewish business, the employees worked half a day on Saturday). She also followed up on possibilities for emigration, both in correspondence and by keeping appointments. Her evenings were interrupted by phone conversations to lawyers about legal points she barely understood, and cared even less about, and she made several trips from Mülheim to Düsseldorf to see them personally, for which she had to keep asking her boss for time off. Though he had turned into a most appreciative and obliging employer who offered to help re-establish my father in business once he was a free man, my mother always had to make up for missed hours on the job.

The maddening thing was that my father knew he'd brought the business fiasco on them both.

After my mother had, not for the first time, conveyed her frustration with the ever increasing complexities of the patent case, and after having told my father that any further expenditure on lawyers was tantamount to throwing good money after bad, my father applied for, and received permission from the prison authorities to write to the relevant parties himself. Though this cleared up some matters for a while, the lawyers turned to my mother again during the weeks in which my father was forbidden from writing.

My mother continued to write weekly, despite having to wait for feedback. She proudly announced she'd received a bonus at work, and was anticipating a permanent salary increase, in recognition of her extra responsibilities, which included being consulted by her boss on every important decision. She chatted on about the boss's sister, *the old crow,* and reported on her own good health, always enquiring after my father's; the weather always got a mention–it hadn't stopped raining for four weeks–and she described the patent imbroglio in ever more sarcastic language; *the topic which I adore and the dearly beloved matter* or *a cute little letter* [from the litigant] *turned up this week* often popped up and reminded me that this was often the droll way she spoke. She also mentioned that she'd shortly be sending my grandfather a pair of socks she'd knitted because she knew he liked the feel of them, a gesture which deeply delighted my father. The elderly man soon reciprocated by sending my mother some "healthy comestibles" for her twenty-fifth birthday.

As soon as my father was allowed to write again in mid-October he announced that his hearing was due to take place in the middle of January 1937, more than a year after he'd been arrested. For some reason, the case would be heard in Berlin, and since he knew my mother had never been there he wrote:

> ...what a way to see the world! I'm delighted that you'll get to see Berlin this way.

My father's incarceration might have been protecting him from knowing about the anti-Semitism prevalent in Berlin when, in fact, the capital city had been persecuting Jews from the time Hitler first came to power. But it may also have been the case that, since the media was tightly controlled and manipulated, what was actually happening to Jews in any part of the country was difficult to determine.

My father claimed he was looking forward to his main hearing with composure, though self-pity had evidently caught up with him since he felt moved to tell my mother he would not stand in her way if she decided she could no longer wait for him.

> I already release my beloved sweetheart from her promise today because it is impossible to pre-determine either fate or circumstances.

That he arrived at such a point is not surprising, given his self-doubting character, yet is astounding considering the exemplary way in which my mother constantly reassured him of her love. Perhaps, therefore, his offer can best be understood as one from a young man who confessed to making grave errors of judgment and causing those closest to him to suffer, but who had matured to manhood and now felt the only honorable thing to do was to let my mother go. Her reply must have bolstered his faltering ego:

Mülheim, 21ˢᵗ November 1936

It took a while until I understood what genuine and profound love was, because I was cautious when it came to "falling in love"...but now my beloved Fidichen, what has taken root in me is deeply rooted; I can never stop loving you. You mean everything to me.

Having received her unqualified response my father prayed:

May the Almighty ordain that we will be reunited, if not for the first anniversary of our marriage, then for the second.

My mother again expressed her own take on things:

What I don't want to think about is our first wedding anniversary. Things that might be able to have an unpleasant effect on me I eliminate provisionally. I'm really good at this! I go to work and come back home with my eyes wide open and yet I see nothing...

I wondered, after three years of Hitlerism, if my mother was hinting at things that were going on in the streets of Mülheim, inimical to Jews, which she chose, for the moment, to ignore. But she described a friend's plan to return to Germany from the US due to overwhelming homesickness, as *clueless and downright stupid.*

By the middle of December my mother's exhortations to my father to remain strong and steadfast, which she repeated with only minor variations in a number of consecutive letters, seemed to indicate that she felt my father needed even more bolstering the closer he got to the main hearing.

Despite her protestations to the contrary, the number of times my mother begged my father to be brave suggested that the impending trial was causing her immense dread. She was also anxiously awaiting news from my grandfather, who had been allowed a pre-trial visit to see his son. Recalling how upset he had become on a previous prison visit my mother wrote:

I do hope the two of you were resolute and firm, as befits men.

Halle, 13th December 1936

Dear Father has just visited me and I am still entirely under the spell of the emotion that such a reunion brings with it. Although we were very composed and manly, it is hard for both sides because each one senses that the other is distraught.

My mother's comment a week later is not particularly convincing and yet it is in keeping with the character I knew so well.

...that you are still under the spell of the emotion of the reunion is something that I can only partially understand... I'm a different sort of person and I think in a completely different fashion. My particularly rational outlook...is innate and unusually advantageous...

Continuing his 13th December letter, my father supplied vignettes of his daily life, which, according to the Halle Memorial curator, consisted of some sort of office work and filing. Additionally:

Every day we are drilled in exercise in the courtyard, the food is completely vegetarian and from the purely physical point of view I have never in my life felt better.

However, conspicuous by its absence is a mention of my father's emotional state which I'm certain did not escape my mother's attention.

He said he was particularly delighted to hear that she was planning a trip to my grandfather's home for Christmas.

Please do put your intention into practice so that you can bring a little bit of happiness to our Father's home.

My mother travelled to Kulmbach on a trip she sarcastically described as a *Himmelfahrt,* a "journey to heaven," because she missed a connecting train, keeping her on the road for nineteen solid hours.

I arrived on Thursday morning at about 7:30 and then spent the entire day and night sleeping.

About Kulmbach, she wrote:

Father was so happy and so were the relatives...I was pleasantly surprised how well he looked, and I find that he's grown very stout...you really don't notice his sixty-four summers...As I said, I'm happy to have visited him... everybody positively showered me with kindness...

Evidently, my maternal grandmother was a little put out by the effort her daughter made to go and see her father-in-law.

Mother was even a bit jealous and said 'you don't have to be so giving to your Father-in-law; in general, you're far more attentive to him than to your own Father.'

Responding to what must have been an uncommonly maudlin letter (not in the collection), my mother continues:

"...what a melancholy mood, my dearest one!! Who's so terribly sad, then? You really mustn't let yourself be so distressed because you'll just become unnecessarily agitated allowing such feelings to play on your nerves. I really feel like scolding you when I read that it's me who's making it difficult for you to be in prison. Of course I understand this but I ask you not to think about me too much.

More than thirteen months had passed since the Nazis snatched my father's freedom, and it had been a time of tumultuous developments. My father's statement to the Halle Magistrate's Court had unveiled an involvement with his uncle and his uncle's friend, suspected by the Nazis of being enemies of the National Socialist state, and it looked as though his association with these two men could be the subject of the main hearing. Because my father had mentioned the coming event with foreboding several times, I assumed it would dwarf the previous two hearings in its seriousness.

The fees that my father owed his lawyer–approximately US$4,000 in today's currency–were beyond his ability to pay because of his frozen assets and my mother, on my father's instructions, had to go cap-in-hand to my great grandfather for this huge outlay.

My parents' third reunion in one year was only days away.

From different sides of the country, my mother and grandfather prepared for their trip to Halle since the trial had been moved back there from Berlin with no explanation. Despite my mother being the younger of the two, by far, from what she had said in one of her letters about my grandfather's fondness for having a good cry, it seemed she would need to set the example for self-control.

In one of her last letters before setting out from Mülheim she had conveyed to my father that she was taking care of the clothes he would wear on the all important day.

I'll be sending you your suit and the underwear you want in the next few days.

I'm wondering whether prisoners on trial were expected to appear in civilian clothes. Whatever the requirement, his well-tailored suit would have served my father as an external prop, restoring to him, however briefly, a semblance of respectability.

Continuing her 16th January letter, my mother raised an issue I'd thought about often when I tried to visualize my father coping with his long nights in jail.

I've never asked you, my beloved treasure, if you can sleep, because I know perfectly well that you'll tell me, yes, I doze and I'll say what is the point of taking a sedative? I know you just as well as I know myself. You used to lie awake when others lay there snoring and sleeping like a log, and today–! Let's not talk about that.

The passage intrigued me, because she'd been married to my father so briefly before he was taken away, yet she was writing like someone who knew his sleeping habits intimately. She may have been referring to the years my father spent in boarding school sleeping in large dormitories filled with snoring youth.

In any event, my father suffered lifelong insomnia, possibly, even as a child, which undoubtedly worsened in prison. He didn't possess my mother's gift for "filing away" problems that threatened his peace of mind. Night after night, on a rock hard bunk in a dank and cheerless prison cell, he'd have nursed (and cursed) his debilitating affliction, fearing that despite his relative youth, it would interfere with his resistance to withstand the ordeal.

As in the case of their first reunion, my mother's letter immediately following the main hearing made no mention of what had transpired in the court. Instead, she spent a considerable part of her letter chatting, yet again, about her job, the boss, and his sister. However, one of the differences between this hearing and the previous two, was that this time my parents had been given permission to speak; the first words they'd spoken to each other in more than a year, though it took her a fortnight and two more letters to mention it (unless there are letters missing). There was no indication as to where in the prison they were allowed to speak. My mother's letter three days after the trial suggests part of the conversation:

Mülheim, 1ˢᵗ February 1937

...You see, my angel, I've never asked whether you still love me or hold me in high regard and whether you still respect me. I tell myself either you do, or I wouldn't have lost anything valuable...I'm thinking here, in particular, of the questions you asked me...I swore to love and remain faithful to you forever, until death us do part, and that includes high esteem and reverence as well. The Devil himself could drive between us and I will never stop loving and appreciating you, you see my beloved all of this just means: I love you!

The long months of separation had nibbled away at my father's self respect, despite my mother's constant reassurances that he was her hero:

I admire and love life's heroes; you my dearest one, I idolize.

<u>Be really steadfast</u> and again I ask you to do me this favor. I promise you today that I'll repay you a thousand times over. On the face of it you have remained the "old fellow," but I'd love to peek into your little heart just once. The main thing I have to find fault with is your posture. You really did stand over me very bent, like a question mark. So chest out, my sweetie-pie! Stand up straight!

Since their letters to each other continued, my father was obviously not set free. The charges, however, remained a mystery:

Halle, 7th February 1937

As all of you know, don't you, I myself am greatly responsible for my own fate...but I can assure you that this coming period will be at most a quarter as difficult as what I've lived through so far.

As I've said, you really don't need to worry your head at all now, about the stupid things I've done in the past. I can promise you one thing: that when all is said and done, I can act sensibly as well. I don't have a lot of sympathy for myself and I must admit I reproach myself quite often... the reproaches are the worst thing, especially if you can scarcely come up with any excuses for your behavior.

I also know there's no point in brooding over things because in life there are no paths back to the past. One has to accept things patiently until one regains one's integrity. You know, my darling, how things look in my heart, don't you? I believe that the heart remains the same always, but the lessons one draws from life and from one's own self have become greater and more valuable. For you my little wife, I have become more interesting and for me you have become even more than you ever were.

I have as good as lost everything, business, assets and freedom; all of this comes, goes and comes again: the biggest gain and the only one in my life is you, my treasure, and this gladdens my heart: that's what keeps me going the whole time.

In a few days I'll finish up-something I never could have dreamed of-in penitentiary.

This letter reverberates with the initial shock of my father's arrest and imprisonment. I find it to be one of the most touching and revealing letters of a young man, who, in cruel and hostile circumstances not of his own making, has grown to maturity, so much so that his past behavior puzzles him.

I assumed that penitentiary was the place in which my father would serve the sentence that was handed down at the main hearing. Only much later did I actually discover the implications of his new "home."

In his poignant soul-searching, my father seemed prepared to absolve the National Socialist court, and to take the full blame for whatever had happened fairly and squarely onto his own shoulders.

During his later life in Australia he displayed a consistently similar leniency in his attitude towards the Nazis whenever there was a social discussion of Nazi crimes. My father would always adamantly maintain that the Allies bore the major responsibility for not acting when they could have and in these exchanges he was always in a minority of one.

> How am I doing this year in terms of mood compared with the same time last year? I admit that I suffered terribly...you, my darling will condemn me later for this, but trust me my sweetheart, you only know a fraction of my "heroic deeds." A year ago, in the same cell, one floor higher up, in comparison my current condition is as if one has gone from hell to paradise.

At some time in my life at home with my parents, probably in my teens, my father, in a context I cannot recall, mentioned that he had purposefully misbehaved in prison suspecting that what would follow his release would be unimaginably worse. I had no idea what he was talking about and furthermore, his declaration frightened me so greatly, I could not pursue the conversation. I now wonder, was he referring to his "heroic deeds?" I didn't even know at the time that my father had been in a Nazi prison. Noemi and I had heard rumors of concentration camp but prison was never mentioned.

His comparison of hell with paradise possibly indicated his relief that the year of waiting in dread about the outcome of his main hearing was over. Uncertainty was the worst thing. Not knowing what the next day, or the one after that would bring, kept him from sleep.

Mülheim, 14th February 1937

Your letters have never made me as happy as the last one...I always knew that my gorgeous one is a strong and courageous man...slowly but hopefully, surely and steadily you've also got it...just stay that way then you'll do yourself and perhaps me too an even bigger favor.

Before my father signed off on his long 7th February letter, he had addressed himself to the issue of a pay rise my mother was expecting. She was quite prepared to accept whatever the increase turned out to be, but my father was more ambitious for her. He advised her to put a small ad in the paper and went so far as to suggest a design for it either to get another job or to bring pressure to bear on her boss. In fact, considering his hapless situation, he displayed a mental toughness in his ability to focus on my mother's life and work. He wrote the ad himself, but it seems my mother never placed it.

Seeking position as:

Secretary

Or store manager

Or bookkeeper

Past experience

Manager of payments section of a retail business

Manager of the shipping department of a textile business

Store manager and shipping manager of a textile manufacturing business

Perfect at shorthand, typing, bookkeeping

Age 25, non-Aryan, used to independent commercial tasks

Who's looking for me?

Offers below monthly salary of 200 marks (pointless) will not be considered.

My mother stayed in her job. She did not want to travel more than she already did which seems to indicate that job offers came from places further away than Mülheim. She also mentioned that from a financial point of view she was enjoying free board and lodgings with her parents in addition to having their emotional support.

The inclusion of my mother's non-Aryan status, sad as it is, indicated that the ad was targeted at Jewish employers, only. Worse still is to see the evidence of the extent to which Jews (my father) had internalized the blatant racism of the Hitlerian regime.

During the month my father was not allowed to write he'd been sent to Bernburg, about thirty kilometers north-west of Halle, as a witness in a case he described as "completely inconsequential to me," and been held there in the court prison for three weeks. The nature of the case or my father's connection to it is never mentioned. Upon his return to Halle he was given permission to resume his correspondence.

Halle, 7th March 1937

My adored sweet darling,

So here I am again in unforgettable Halle...I do hope that I'll move into my permanent quarters soon although this could be interrupted since [uncle] Gustav's trial hasn't been fixed yet and I might have to go to Berlin as a witness. It really doesn't make any difference where I am,

since in terms of "board and lodgings" it's the
same everywhere.

The reference to his uncle Gustav's trial confirmed that Dr.
Flörsheim had also been arrested and, apparently, was being held
in Berlin.

My father's tongue-in-cheek, self-deprecating reference to
Halle and his living quarters, hints at the quiet inner strength–
sometimes perceived as weakness, at other times overlooked
because of his tendency to be indecisive–of a modest young man
who had adjusted to the trauma of his arrest and imprisonment and
to the fear and uncertainty about the outcome of a court hearing
conducted by Nazis.

In Bernburg, as you know, I was allowed to
continue my language studies for the sake of my
further education and subsequent livelihood...
my dear little one, keep your fingers crossed
for me that this permission will be given later
too, in the penitentiary...there were periods in
Bernburg when the day passed too fast for me, I
was so industrious in my [intellectual] efforts;
in actual fact, of course no minute passes fast
enough in order to "soon" return to my little
heart's desire, and when you get this letter,
it'll all be going downhill with my detention...

Eleven days later my father would complete his six-month
sentence.

In her letter before the main hearing, my mother had begun a
discussion about grieving in order to reassure my father that she
was coping with their tragedy publicly as well as privately.

My father replied:

You write, my beloved lass, that there are people in Mülheim who question that 50% of my burden in captivity is offset by the fact that my noble little wife doesn't wear her heart on her sleeve and makes no secret of her divinely strong soul and her naturally joyful disposition...but I thank God that He created you, my sweetheart, the way you are.

My mother denied any grief at all:

Mülheim, 20th March 1937

The thing that I like best is the way I am easing your burden by 50% and if you think that I'm displaying any grief publicly let me put the record straight: I'm not grieving at all, neither publicly nor privately. But now things are proceeding at the rate of knots, and you must stop grieving too.

As they were heading towards the finish line their assurances to one another, while they remained ever positive, also grew more urgent. My mother's comment about *things proceeding at the rate of knots* and a little later her remark about being *carried on towards [their] happiness* and my father's mention that it'll all be going downhill with [his] detention gave the unmistakable impression that neither could contain their desperation to be reunited.

After no mention of the subject for seven months, my father once again enquired about emigration:

Has my affidavit of support arrived yet? For how long is it valid? Has something been undertaken for you too?

My mother replied:

Your affidavit of support hasn't arrived yet, and won't be arriving for the time being. Anyway, there's plenty of time for that, because what point would there be in allowing the period for going to the consulate to expire without deriving any benefit from it.

It seems my father was destined to remain a prisoner for the foreseeable future. Nevertheless, my mother had attended to the emigration issue as promised, resulting in my father's American cousins proposing that she emigrate by herself. My father encouraged that idea but she was adamantly opposed. Did she know that my father's freedom would become her sole responsibility?

There cannot be any question of me going without you. But we haven't got to that stage yet, so let's just keep our cool.

My father's well-meaning American cousins, whom I met in 1971, seemed unable to grasp how dire the situation in Germany had become for Jews, especially for those like my father who were trapped inside Nazi jails.

Changing tack, my mother makes the second and last reference to saving their letters, those precious missives which were all she had of her husband, each one that reached her signaling that he was alive. This time she explains to my father their meaning and future value.

Keep these letters safe as I do too, so that we'll always have the opportunity to prove to each other our mutual love, intense adoration and affection in writing.

She views the letters as the written proof of the power of love sustained in distressing and dangerous circumstances…*that which* *fills the heart...*She is not thinking of the suffering and heartache they contain or that they are the evidence of gross injustices committed against Jews during a period of incomparable anti-Semitism. To her, they are simply expressions of love that survived their inhospitable surroundings.

Later, the very fact that they never mentioned their existence either to Noemi or me, suggests that the letters came to represent a sad and painful era in their lives best left in the past. Nevertheless, they did not destroy them, leaving them to be discovered, presumably, after their deaths.

In her next letter she returned to some light relief:

Mülheim, 28th March 1937

...as soon as we've made some progress at work, I'll inadvertently be ill for one to two days with a touch of lazyitis. I'm sure you just don't get that, do you my Fidichen? But hang on a moment I've just remembered that you did this sort of thing too. I heard at work that you were ill, and I rushed out and brought you a little flower. Who wasn't at home when the visitor to the sick turned up? My cute Gottfried. Another case of lazyitis?

I'd often wondered where in Mülheim my parents lived in relation to one another. Noemi and I knew that Bachstrasse 62 was my mother's address, but my father never mentioned his, perhaps wanting to avoid any questions about that period in his life. By a stroke of good luck in 2007 while sorting through some of my mother's papers after she died, Noemi came across a small, thin book resembling a passport labeled "Arbeitsbuch," my father's record of employment with his name and address on it–Althofstrasse 42–listed on the inside. With the help of the

Internet it took only minutes to pinpoint Althofstrasse on a map of the inner city of Mülheim showing that it was about three hundred meters from Bachstrasse. This seemed the most likely location for the consummation of their relationship and the place where my mother jokingly threatened to pad the corners of the room in anticipation of a pre-wedding wrestling match with my father upon his return from abroad.

A week after hatching her plan for a case of "lazyitis" my mother put it into action.

I spent a day skiving on Wednesday...and I just relaxed. On Thursday morning I told [the boss] tales from A Thousand and One Nights, and the dozy fellow swallowed the lot.

By 18th March 1937, my father had completed serving his six-month sentence. A Dr. Knauf, presumably his lawyer, contacted my mother to tell her that my father had been moved to penitentiary to begin serving his second sentence handed down at the main hearing, news my mother received in a positive frame of mind:

Mülheim, 25th April 1937

If I think ahead a bit, and by then, PG we'll be together in good health, I'll be the happiest person on earth and I wouldn't want to change places with anyone. My thoughts are running ahead a little too much now...and we're getting closer and closer to the time when we'll be happy.

Of course I'll come for the first visiting day on 19th June... Your Father doesn't always need to come, but PG (please God) I'd like to come and see you on every visiting day.

My mother's use of the word "need" puzzled me. She either wanted her husband to herself for once or alternatively, she was being considerate to her elderly father-in-law who would be fatigued by a long train journey.

I've suggested to [your] Father that we visit you together in June. First of all, I've got to do all sorts of sewing for myself and a lot of work, and secondly I'd like to catch up on my sleep. This isn't a period when I can take any time off, and it's a real schlep for two days. Whether we see each other four weeks earlier or later makes practically no difference. It's also not nice to travel in this weather.

Captured in the above extract is my mother's familiar determination to arrange matters in a practical fashion. Having her affairs, her belongings and her immediate environment in order were always high priorities. Yet to be fair, the long months of waiting, plus the arrivals and departures at the prison, must have been a constant emotional drain despite her protestations to the contrary.

Since it's your Father's birthday next week, I've asked Frau Weber what he could do with, since it's nicer not to give things that people don't need. This way, he's going to get two nice nightshirts from you and from me two light summer combinations and various trifles. That'll do nicely.

Ever since Karl Strauss, a widower of fourteen years, first made his appearance in my parents' correspondence, neither my mother nor my father had mentioned the presence in his life of a female. I therefore guessed that Frau Weber must have been either my grandfather's cleaning lady or housekeeper since she seemed to know him well enough for my mother to be able to consult her about his wardrobe. In the course of events, Frau Weber would become a familiar figure.

The visit scheduled for 19th June 1937 was to be a gift for my father's thirtieth birthday four days earlier. My mother assured him that it would be the last birthday of its kind since, for his thirty-first, there would be *love afresh-newly invigorated* which indicated that by June 1938, they expected my father to be released. In her next letter, she prepared the emotional ground for the forthcoming meeting:

Mülheim, 9th May 1937

If I come with [your] Father, you're going to have to be really strong. You know I don't like to see tears. Be my brave hero and stay that way.

And a week later:

But you must promise me you won't get worked up when we visit you. I remember that you once wrote to me, when [your] Father came to visit you, you enjoyed it when he came–but when he left!!! So please my dear Gottfried, just this once, be like me and in this case don't forget that after all it's just a set period of time that separates you from us.

Always careful to include news of my grandfather and be the reliable go-between, my mother added:

Thank God he's fine and he was so delighted with the things we sent that he's thinking of returning the favor. But I wrote to him that he shouldn't dare send anything. He was also thrilled with my Mother's present of a tie. That makes me so happy – everything has served its purpose.

And yet again two weeks later:

...in the meanwhile you must prepare yourself, my sweetheart, for my visit and at the same time again for my leaving, just as I'm doing.

My father had already confessed to going through hell behind the scenes but he'd also insisted that he had conquered the worst of his inner turmoil. Did this mean that he'd succeeded in desensitizing himself? The future would tell.

By now my father had been in prison for eighteen months and, during that time, the situation affecting Jews worsened daily. Apparently, this information filtered into prisons.

Halle, 30th May 1937

I've received dear Father's letter. I'm concerned about a recent decree that would soon make it possible to legally revoke the practicing of one's profession. If something like that were to come into force, I'd ask him not to wear himself down – in a year from now I'll again be in a position where we'll be able to survive and then we'll have him come and live with us.

Such decrees were implemented soon after Hitler's rise to power with academics, doctors and lawyers being some of the first professionals affected. However, those decrees excluding Jews from the German economy, per se, came later. The situation started to worsen in 1937 with more Aryanization of private Jewish businesses; since my grandfather worked in the family's cattle trading business my father was most likely referring to one of those economic boycotts.

> I am of the firm belief that I'll have [my] money
> released, just as I'm absolutely convinced that
> sooner or later I will regain control over what
> is mine and belongs to me.

My father's belief in the ultimate justice of The Third Reich was a misjudgment of immense proportions, but not at all uncommon. National Socialism was perceived by many to be a passing phenomenon that would soon be replaced by popular demand. Not until Germany's defeat at the end of WWII did the Germans introduce a system of reparations and compensations but it's unclear what period my father was referring to.

There remained anomalies in the system. While the Nazis robbed Jews of their livelihood and possessions, in penitentiary my father was still receiving money my mother regularly sent him. The other side of this coin is to see it as self-interest. Whatever relatives supplied to inmates, was less bother for the prison.

In answer to my mother's pleas to observe decorum at their next reunion my father displayed an unusual boldness:

> As far as my own state of health is concerned,
> all I will say is: Come, see and be amazed. If,
> my courageous lass, you want to preclude any
> shedding of tears, this is an item which I have
> long since put on one side...one can get used to
> anything so easily, to beautiful things as well
> as to bad things.

The longer I worked with the letters the more I came to admire my father's steely, though entirely unassuming will to prevail. The techniques he presumably used to inure himself to emotional vulnerability never blocked access later on to the warmth of his personality and his readiness to empathize with others, despite nursing lifelong scars:

> You wrote to me back in March last year that the blows inflicted by fate had left their marks on [your Mother's] appearance. Are things still as bad now? I do hope that when I see her again, I'll find the same old unshakeable Mother.

> The best time-keeper (without his watch) is always when I am allowed to write to you. Eight weeks have passed and they've gone very quickly for me; when at 1 o'clock after I've got down to my light duties and beaver away so I can get through my daily quota, I sometimes think it must be getting on for 2 o'clock and the clock strikes 4 and I am absolutely amazed as well as pleased how time flies.

In her letters leading up to their meeting on Sunday 20th June my mother continued to write about her boss, his sister–*the clumsy old oaf*–the weather, the patent business, her love of sleeping and her refusal to be or look miserable. Some of the letters are unusually short considering her writing space was not restricted like my father's. In any event, despite the fact that she'd postponed their meeting by about a month it was clear she was anxious to see her husband.

Her ever-increasing desperation for my father to remain healthy to the date of exit was clear. The situation would become ruinous if he took ill. If they stayed in Germany, finding work as Jews would be problematic if not impossible, and if they needed to flee it would make traveling difficult. With all her might she prayed that my father would remain strong to the end.

May the dear Lord make this an untroubled reunion insofar as it's a healthy one. God willing, Dad and I will turn up on 20th June.

On 15th June, my father reached his thirtieth birthday with only the written wishes from my mother to mark the day.

With God's help we'll celebrate the next birthday together… my warmest congratulations and many happy returns.

Their June meeting was rapturous. It made my mother swoon and write that she lacked the words to express how it had moved her. Yet she did quite well when she wrote that she felt *rich,* was transported *to higher regions* and that *there's a smile on my lips the whole time.* She was delighted to see that my father still had that *sweet boyish face,* adding that *dear old Dad is absolutely thrilled at how you're conducting yourself, and once again encloses his letter.*

The joy and relief at hearing that my father was well also extended itself to my grandmother:

My dear Gottfried,

Since you always get my regards through Irene, for once I want to send you my love in person. And I always think of you with love.

With all my best love in my thoughts,

[Your] Mother

Who loves you.

Towards the end of the letter my mother wrote:

I'm fine and with such a splendid constitution I'd love to live to be a hundred; naturally, only under your beloved protection and that, my darling won't take too much longer.

My mother's expressed wish to live to be a century, but only with my father by her side, brought back memories of the turbulence caused by his sudden death when she was sixty-eight, struggling to live a life without him for the second time.

Ten days later my mother entertained my father with the continuing shenanigans at her work:

Mülheim, 7th July 1937

I'm practically always on a war footing with [the boss's] sister...even though she's 50, the old girl still has ideas which really don't suit her age. For example, she pinned a piece of brightly colored cretonne on my (cloth) coat and that's how I went off to the railway station. This wouldn't be so bad if she did her work properly, but she wastes a lot of time on nonsense like this and makes messes which I have to sort out. This is time I'd rather spend playing with my big fat toe...last week she poured some water (that she thought smelled nice) on my overall which was enough to make one feel quite sick. I held the overall under the boss's nose and he was practically overcome. What do you think of such goings on?

My father thought the story so droll that [he] had to laugh out loud.

After two months, on 1st August 1937, my father expressed his feelings about my mother's earlier visit:

When I returned to my cell 6 weeks ago today, my sweet little Tutti had made me quite euphoric...I really cannot express how delightful you looked in your lovely outfit. Your taste is exquisite...

what a delicious foretaste and after taste [these
visits] have; I'm happy 3 months in advance and
the impressions last practically unaltered for 3
months...it is a great relief for me to be able
to see your dear face every so often even for just
10 minutes. I was delighted to see Father looking
so well and will, please God, see you both again
in 6 weeks time.

For this fleeting encounter my mother had to travel the five hundred kilometers there and back; for my grandfather, Kulmbach to Halle was about half the distance. Nevertheless, at age sixty-four it was a tiring journey. It seemed an inordinately short visiting time until Michael Viebig, the Halle Memorial curator, explained that the visiting booths were a ten-minute walk from the visitor's registration desk. A walk there and back reduced the available visiting time to one third of thirty minutes. In any event, I'm certain my mother and grandfather would have settled for thirty seconds just to see that my father was all right. Every moment counted. My father wrote:

I recommend that given the short visiting time,
you make notes of the most important things that
you want to tell me about. That's what I always do
if there are a number of important points that I
don't want to forget...I now have left just under
a third of my time.

This announcement roughly coincided with my mother's declaration that by June 1938, my father would be free. Though still about ten months away, my mother spoke of *making giant strides towards happiness.* In anticipation, she went and bought a length of fine brown suit material to have made up for my father.

Don't be annoyed and say don't get ahead of yourself. I got a lot of pleasure out of already seeing you in my mind's eye so well dressed and in my opinion you've never owned anything so beautiful and of such good quality.

My father admired my mother for the ease with which she spent money on those she cared for though, in his response, he underestimated her thoughtfulness and came perilously close to looking a gift horse in the mouth:

```
I can say with a clear conscience that there is
hardly anything that has given me more pleasure
than this action which you took in love. Your
choice of color brown very much meets my taste...
but in practical terms for the future perhaps grey
might be better because it is easier to choose
hat, coat, shirt and collar...just by-the-by.
```

And she replied:

So did you think me so impractical, my angel, as to have only one piece of suiting in brown for you? No, my beloved Gottfried, I couldn't stop at one; I've long had a length in the same fabric in grey…

By the beginning of September 1937, my mother had received visitors' permits for the 26th of the month for herself and my grandfather who, in her eyes, had repeated his minor blunder of reminding my father about Jewish New Year. Since my father's attention had already been drawn to the festival, my mother wrote that, on the Day of Atonement, she and her family observed the twenty-four hour fast and all of them had withstood it well. This year my father did not mention whether or not he'd fasted as he'd done in 1936, which made me suspect that his diet was insufficient. Time would tell. In any event, in his previous letter he'd floated the idea of skipping the September visit because of the expense it would incur.

My mother scoffed at the idea of foregoing a visit *for a miserable 35 marks:*

I don't give a hoot about the expense; for my sweetheart nothing is too much! And anyway, it's not just idealism but also egotism.

Her exhilaration was such that she claimed that if the forthcoming visit produced the same degree of euphoria as the previous one *it would be better to put me on a leash, like Bello, because otherwise I'll go around jumping for joy.*

By way of reporting on events in their extended families as my mother often did, she wrote that my grandmother's brother, Fritz, had left Germany and taken his wife and baby to settle in the US. Before Fritz emigrated, my grandmother had all her five siblings living in Germany. However, by the time she and my grandfather arrived in Australia, she, Fritz and her sister Selma, who had also fled to America, were the only three who survived the Holocaust. Oma had been looking forward to being reunited with her brother and sister after the war (her other siblings were never mentioned), but once my father brought our family to Australia and stayed, Oma had to rely on letters to stay in touch and as things transpired she never saw her siblings again.

The relief at finding my father in good health at their 26th September meeting once again transported my mother to new heights of happiness. She was *quite out of [her] mind* and *walking on air.* My grandfather, too, was overjoyed to see *his beloved offspring.* Perhaps because she'd found him looking so well at her two previous visits my mother decided to cut back on her weekly letters and write only once a month, though the real reason is unknown.

For the moment let's keep it at one letter because happiness no longer depends on this.

When she did write again she admitted to a weight gain of three kilos, adding that she was *becoming a right little roly-poly,* which didn't seem to worry her because *being "podgy" helps one through the winter.* My father, who set great store by my mother's looks advising her to use more make-up and let her hair grow, did not, in this instance respond to her recent weight gain. As the months crept by, did reality force him to adopt new priorities? His former preoccupation with her physical appearance might have felt trivial when compared with his gratitude and relief at having a loyal, loving and utterly devoted wife.

The closer my father got to the end of his term the more he seemed to fret about money.

Halle, 29th November 1937

What do you and dear Father think about the idea of <u>him</u> passing next time (on 26th December) and saving on the trip to come and see me and then coming again next year when my sentence is up? I leave this up to you and the dear old fellow. It's true that it's nicer if <u>both</u> of you were to come.

My father continued:

How short life is, how quickly it passes one can see from the last 2 years; how quickly we forget

them, first our wedding; then the arrest and our
reunion in June '36 in Mülheim – this is really
what shattered me most of all things and events
in my entire life, with the exception of when I
got the news about the death of my beloved late
Mother. But at the time I was 16, just a boy, and
last year I was a man who had all kinds of sorrow
behind him. I will never forget this reunion,
because the wound of our separation had largely
healed during the half year of my detention and
my imagination had conjured up a picture of you
which, as always, in reality was far exceeded
by your natural beauty. Moreover, the wound was
ripped open too abruptly since at that time what
was going to happen to me was shrouded in dreadful
uncertainty.

I had long suspected that my father's letters, especially the one after their 5th June 1936 reunion, had put a brave face on what was, in essence, a horrendous ordeal and that his visits with my mother and grandfather had often required supreme play acting. I returned to the letter my father had written immediately after that first reunion and indeed, found there not the slightest hint of the devastation he now says he experienced. In fact, his words were a total cover-up. He had written:

You have no idea what a positive effect seeing
you again had on me...

It had taken him eighteen months to reveal the internal upheaval my mother's first visit in six months had caused him. Confronted with what he'd lost, his emotional defenses collapsed. Yet he'd managed to conceal this trauma for so long.

Five weeks earlier my mother had passed on some news concerning my father's impounded car. She wrote that she'd been intensely annoyed by the authorities who had fined her for not being able to produce the vehicle's registration papers for which she claimed she'd already paid:

They wanted 20 marks because I couldn't produce the papers. I was told you had been questioned about the matter but what could you have known about it since by then you were no longer here. I did pay for the registration about a year ago but I don't remember receiving the document. You can imagine, my sweetheart, that at first I was really cross about the fine, but I got over it quickly due to my sense of humor and I've now calmed down.

In all the years I'd known him I'd never heard my father reproach my mother, but now, he did.

It really annoys me that you paid the fine last year. How can you pay for things that have nothing to do with you, especially in light of the State having taken measures to confiscate both the car and assets? The matter isn't over, my child! If the Ministry doesn't release the money, you'll lay claim to these 20 marks through Dr. Knauf. But you must not under any circumstances now pay again, irrespective of where this registration certificate may be. Please write to me about this and also let me know why you didn't ask me about it.

My father failed to take into account the abnormal circumstances in which he and my mother were operating, where communication was hardly instant like it is with today's technology. Towards the end of 1936, he had been restricted to writing once a month; my mother had begun full time work; she was handling the patent business against her better judgment and she was unwaveringly attentive to my father and grandfather. There were bound to be misunderstandings from lapses in time and memory. Worse still, with the benefit of hindsight, it is shocking to learn of my father's continuing faith in the fairness of the Nazi legal system and the bureaucracy that supported it.

By the time she wrote next on 11th December 1937, my mother had responded to an earlier request of my father's to write to her family in the US in order to increase their chances of acquiring affidavits.

There's nothing that can be done about [my] Father's Brother, my dearest darling…no one will give me the address because they think that they might be put at a disadvantage…Aunty Henny won't write for me either. She, too, went to him years ago about her Sister who was and is in a very bad way and got an answer which she could never have imagined. Since then the matter has been closed.

The Jews of Germany could not foresee what was about to happen to them. Yet, it was distressing to learn, albeit in an inexact manner, that there were relatives who were not prepared to help each other in every possible way. However, since my parents never spoke about these issues and I'd never heard mention of my mother's uncle, the story remains incomplete.

Her letter concluded with the date of the next reunion on 1st January 1938. The day after it my mother wrote from Bielefeld where she'd stopped off to visit a cousin on her return to Mülheim:

My sweet Daddy,

How wonderful it was to see each other again...your lovely words are still going around in my brain and when I think of the divorce business, I feel like doing somersaults and laughing out loud.

A little over a year earlier when my father's main hearing was looming, he had been wracked with doubts about its outcome to such an extent that he thought it only fair to offer my mother a divorce. During the 1st January prison visit when the date of his impending release was drawing closer he again offered to set her free. My mother mocked him mercilessly:

...my dear little Gottfried, think it over again really carefully, and if it's <u>what you want</u> then I'll go back to being a spinster!...In any case I'll wait for your next letter and enquire politely now of my sweetheart whether I may look around for another husband. If applicable, I would have to put an ad in the paper because given my job I have no opportunity to move in circles where marriages could be in the offing!!!...and how's your little tooth my darling? Since I'm still going to pay for it, please, please get it attended to immediately. Please don't wait until the divorce, because then I will no longer pay for you.

On a more sober note my mother reported her family's delight about my father's well-being. My grandfather, she wrote, had visited her family in Mülheim and had been unusually talkative, which she thought was a sign of his growing relief that the ordeal would soon come to an end.

However, much to my mother's chagrin the patent case resurfaced thanks to a new and apparently obnoxious lawyer who summoned her to his office in Düsseldorf. The man bawled her out shamelessly, demanding certain documents she couldn't readily produce. The meeting, she wrote, *had [me] boiling with rage for two weeks.* As soon as she'd collected the papers and sent them to him she announced she would never again see him or speak with him.

If I'd used the 3½ hours I spent with him sleeping instead it would have done me a lot more good…if he wants to know something he should contact you. I'm tired of the whole thing, and that's it.

Judging by my mother's next letter of 3rd February 1938, yet another one from my father is missing from the collection. In it, he evidently *managed to see the funny side* of her rage and correctly guessed that she wasn't feeling as nasty as she had made out. His accurate perception prompted her, once again, to draw comparisons between their personalities:

People of your type…suffer unspeakably when fate deals them a cruel blow, but on the other hand experience good and beautiful things with such enjoyment that they can live off them for a long time afterwards. Natures like mine are unemotional and practically immune to major trials and tribulations, as tough as old boots, and if in addition they have a skin as thick as I've been able to grow with G-d's help in the last 2 years or so, then TG everything slides off just like water off a duck's back.

Switching once again to a breezier mood she took nine lines to discuss her new hairdo. In response to a relative's criticism that short hair was making her look too masculine, she let it grow and combed it up into a roll which would have pleased my father who was always trying to encourage her to wear her hair long. She commented:

And you, my darling, care so much about appearances...

On 27th February 1938, my father devoted his entire four-page tightly-written letter to the new lawyer who had been rude to my mother. Since the gentleman had been unable to read my father's handwriting, my father asked my mother to faithfully copy the letter and send it on to him. The letter consists of my father's descriptions of financial deals that had been struck with employees of the firm, payments made, commissions earned, rights sold or held, arguments that had raged and negotiations that had fallen through. My mother was mentioned several times as a witness to certain business meetings but beyond these observations it was impossible to make sense of my father's letter. My mother was hoping that he would be released in time to be personally present at the court hearing so that the patent wrangle could be settled once and for all, since she could *neither make head nor tail of it.*

If all references to my father's date of release were correct, it seemed fair to assume that the 27th March 1938 prison visit would be the last of nine times my mother and father saw each other in approximately two and a half years. My mother emerged from that visit *elated.* Was my father's release only weeks away?

Halle, 3rd April 1938

My beloved Tutti,

I was looking forward to this last visit of yours and Father's with mixed feelings, because I thought I'd have to send home an Irene whose unhappiness would be just as great when she left as her happiness was when she came dashing in but I was wrong: not that I assumed that you didn't have the faintest idea about how things are, but I presumed that the two of you aren't quite in the picture about my situation.

It would really be stupid not to have learned by now to come to terms with everything... Unfortunately, in my case, it took a very long time until my sensibilities became fairly dulled, as you may have noticed.

What would you say if I were to tell you that I've already known for 2 years that there is a possibility of additional confinement pending investigation. I've really known this for 4 years now, because while other people manage to forget in blissful slumber that which torments their consciousness during the day, I've always lain awake, just suffering twice as much.

The only way to explain the apparent contradiction in my father's letter is to assume he knew, or was told, after his first hearing in Mülheim on 5th June 1936 about the possibility of additional confinement pending investigation. The fact that he then goes on to claim that he really knew of this possibility four years earlier might indicate he had heard about it from others long before he was arrested.

> This suffering, the sleeplessness, that I endured for years even before I was arrested, is actually the real reason for my entire fate from A-Z, including the acts of desperation in detention which today I find incomprehensible. This suffering sucks the blood from a man's heart and mind, weakening his energy and willpower, disrupting his ability to think and remember.

No matter how often I read my father's 3rd April 1938 letter, I continued to be baffled by his reference to his "acts of desperation," never taking into account that he was a young man prone to the inevitable mistakes of youth. I knew my father as thoughtful, measured in his ways and slow to make decisions. But reading of his apparently impulsive behavior I recalled a random remark he once made to me in a long forgotten context when I was about twelve.

> I misbehaved in prison knowing what was coming afterwards, would be much worse.

He did not elaborate then or at any time and I, startled and frightened, asked no questions. In those few seconds I understood he had been in prison, and that "afterwards" must have referred to concentration camp.

I don't know whether this comment and my father's other one-liners were intended to provoke enquiries that would lead to an open discussion. What I'm sure of is that his occasional allusions to dreadful events in his past inevitably cast a shadow over family life.

In any event, in this final surviving letter from Halle, his second sentence almost served, my father sums up the last two and a quarter years. His words are convoluted and sometimes frustratingly contradictory. They are also sad since they come from the heart of an agonized soul. After his main hearing my father took responsibility for what had happened to him; now, again, he expresses culpability without ever implying that the entire fiasco of his arrest and imprisonment was the result of being caught in an evil regime that had turned against its Jews. Of course, he could not say that because of censorship but I tend to believe he would have seen the regime as a secondary cause of his misfortune and not the primary one. Then again, he blames his longstanding insomnia for all his woes and misadventures.

My father provides no background in his 3rd April 1938 letter, or at any other time, to the origins of his condition. However, there were enough horrid things happening in German society that would have preyed on his mind. These included the ninety laws Hitler passed restricting the rights of Jews to make a living in the two years before my father was taken prisoner, developments which in themselves would have ruined my father's nights. Other causes of his insomnia, pre-dating the steep rise in anti-Semitism, are probably related to inflation, an economic disaster that struck terror in my father's heart.

Yet, the worst of his disclosures is that on the due date of his release, 11th May 1938, there is a question mark hanging over his freedom. Furthermore, he claims he has known about this probability all along and suggests my mother and grandfather might have suspected it, too.

His words recalled a comment in his 20th September 1936 letter about going back into protective custody even if he were acquitted in the main hearing unless my mother was able to secure an affidavit, which now made more sense. And my father's offer to divorce my mother after his main hearing also suggested that he knew of the real possibility of further detention.

During the Nazi years, being taken into protective custody after imprisonment usually meant being sent to concentration camp, but I didn't fully comprehend the relationship between Nazi prisons and the Nazi law courts until further research provided some solid answers.

Already in 1933, the German Ministries of Justice in different German states were ordering prison governors to report the upcoming release of certain political prisoners, thereby ensuring the concentration camps with a steady stream of inmates, and by January 1937, the month of my father's main hearing, the Reich Ministry of Justice ordered penal institutions to report these prisoners to the Gestapo one month before their release. My father must have known this as he indicates in his 3rd April 1938 letter, but did my mother know?

> I must say that I am unable to look forward as eagerly to 11th May, as some serious offender looks forward to the end of his sentence, and as long as 2 years ago I was already more afraid of my sentence coming to an end than of any verdict by the court...I had already lost any belief of ever again coming back healthy. Do you now have some understanding of the profound emotions that shook me to my core in June '36 as I faced my sweet little unsuspecting Tutti?

My father's letter continued:

> And yet I can assure you that most of the time I am extremely glad that my imprisonment is over, not

only because today I am no longer convinced of any
additional confinement pending investigation, but
because one way or another my life will be better
than here and in a situation like this, a person
is, you know, so grateful for any improvement to
his life, particularly if it is nothing but a
staging post to eventual freedom...but what would
freedom be for me today without you...who's so
brave and prepared to stick with me through thick
and thin...if I do finish up in protective custody
my hair will have a lot more time to grow.

Incidentally, this [protective] custody can be
demanded by the Oberhausen or Halle Police, by
the Director of Public Prosecutions, but always
requires the confirmation of the Reichsführer-SS,
Heinrich Himmler.

The letter made my head swim with its statements seemingly
at variance with one another, and seeing Himmler's name in my
father's letter made me feel ill. Yet now I was clear on the terrifying
implications of "protective custody" and "additional confinement
pending investigation." Also, I was astonished that particularly the
remainder of the letter passed censorship.

If the Central Verein is able to undertake some
action on my behalf they will have to be extremely
careful about how they word the application. I
want to tell you the following. There must be
no indication of my desire to emigrate because
someone has stood surety for me so that I can
avoid additional confinement pending investigation

and this bond will be withdrawn if I indicate my desire to emigrate. Not only would this contradict the facts but it would also be dangerous.

Please tell the CV that the only way the application can be drafted is as follows: since in general the emigration of Jews is desired, and since for me, personally, there will probably be no possibility of earning a living after my release, is my emigration still desired and expected by the competent state authorities?

My father's sheer terror at the mere possibility of angering the Nazis by the use of a wrong word or phrase is sickening. Yet it seems that the correct and precise wording of his enquiry was absolutely necessary. No matter how many times I read it, this letter never failed to enrage me by the way one supposedly had to grovel to the authorities, covertly begging for one's life and freedom.

The approach to the Central Verein, The General Association of German Citizens of Jewish Faith to which my father was alluding, was an organization that tried to help Jews cope with growing anti-Semitism.

Less than a month earlier my father had been eager for news about his affidavit from the US; now his parole complicated matters:

In other words, I really do not want to [emigrate], but would only if the competent State authorities want me to. This is what *must* be expressed. If the surety bond has not yet arrived, the application

must be submitted together with a note that it is
on its way.

My mother chose to address emotional issues, cleverly avoiding
the sensitive topic of emigration in all but the most general of
terms at the end of her letter.

Mülheim, 21ˢᵗ April 1938

*...you thought you'd see an Irene come charging in happily.
I'm always happy when I think of you and even more when
I can see you...you don't tell me anything new whatsoever
when you talk about your insomnia and feelings. I know
you so well, after all, and precisely because of that I respect
you and hold you in high esteem and love you far, far more
than I did before...I've imagined everything, everything the
way you describe it. So carry on being as strong as an ox...
sometimes with the best will in the world I cannot understand
everything that you've been imagining in the past years.
However much you've thought about things, you can never
have reached any result. I'm far less complicated than you
when it comes to thinking...*

*What it means, freedom without Tutti — I just can't understand.
But you do have me, my sweetie-pie, and as long as I'm
alive, you'll always have me. Perhaps later on it will even
be to your regret!!*

My mother's self-mocking wit endured into her eighties even
after her loss of short-term memory.

Almost at the end of the letter my mother deals with what, I assume, my father was most anxious to hear:

As far as the main thing in your letter is concerned, you can be entirely reassured I've been given enough good advice to last me till 1940. Everything that's been requested is being dealt with.

My mother's penultimate (existing) letter from my father's time in Halle dated 3rd May 1938, seems to indicate yet another missing letter:

I'm sure you've received both my letters from last month [April] when in fact there is only one in the collection from April 1938. Nevertheless, since she'd written that she was attending to all that my father had asked, this last but final letter once again addressed itself to the minutiae of everyday life, including my grandfather's sixty-fifth birthday for which he was again to receive from my mother *a cotton sports shirt and other little tokens of affection… together with a birthday kiss.* She followed this with a whole paragraph on her hair:

The only thing I'm not satisfied with is my hair. The mop is growing so slowly and I can't pull it with force into the length I want. After I subjected it to a wash I looked like some disheveled creature.

The letter ended with a description of my grandmother, indisposed by a knee complaint:

…Mother has had an inflamed knee for 11 weeks now…But in all these weeks she's not neglected her household, even if things aren't quite as ship-shape as she would like…In her own way she's like a child. 2 months ago I wanted her to

go to hospital, but nothing doing. Mothers are terrible, they think they're indispensable; am I going to be like that?

In reply to my mother's rhetorical question, the answer is a resounding yes. Like her mother she was slavishly devoted to her household duties.

If she hadn't put any strain on the knee the inflammation would have cleared in 3 weeks but she insisted on doing her work in the mornings and only rests the knee in the afternoon. So what gets better in the afternoon is spoiled again the next day which is why I help out in the evenings and prepare things just so that she can rest more.

The grand finale to the Mülheim-Halle-Kulmbach correspondence ends with a letter written jointly by my grandfather and mother when he went to visit my mother's family after my father's expected date of release. Up until now, my grandfather's character had been conveyed through my parents' comments but in the letter he co-wrote with my mother he expresses himself directly.

My grandfather's handwriting, in Old Gothic Sütterlin script, covers three-quarters of a yellowing page and bears a brownish vertical and horizontal stain intersecting in the middle where it has been folded. Though its contents are not easily accessible, I treasure the letter.

In the top left hand corner, running a short way down the page, someone had scribbled a list of words which at first I couldn't decipher. My guess is they were written by my father.

Handkerchiefs

Passport politically confiscated

Relief Organization urgent

Sickness

Uncle Abraham sponsor parole

Small suitcase

Direct Immigration

Consulate

Tickets ship

Tourist

Armed with the facts I'd gathered so far I fancied composing a drama based on the points listed, convinced that, even with scant regard for the truth, I could create a tale of high adventure. As things developed, I had no need to resort to invention.

On 11th May 1938 a Friday, my grandfather appeared at Halle jail to collect his son and with him, cross the portals of the prison for the last time.

When he arrived at police headquarters, however, he was informed that his son would not be released for the time being, and furthermore, that he couldn't see him because it wasn't an official visiting day. He was told he could apply for a visitor's permit for ten days hence. Before leaving, my grandfather asked if he could send my father some food parcels but that, apparently, was also forbidden. Soon after, he had traveled on to Mülheim to convey the bad news to my mother and her family in person. While he was there, he wrote to my father.

13th May 1938
...I was told that you are allowed to buy food for yourself but that we are not allowed to send you any. If you need money, write to me because when we last saw you over six weeks ago your appearance

gave us cause for concern. Therefore, we are going to request a suspension of further imprisonment and parole. The Relief Organization tells us they could take care of your emigration on the condition that the authorities agree to it and your condition allows it.

All our dear ones are in good health and get pleasure from each other. With the help of G-d, I will return home on Sunday.

I hope to receive a letter from you soon and remain with heartfelt kisses,

Your Father who loves you.

Father

I was relieved to see that my grandfather, whose fatalism I had questioned earlier, had taken matters into his own hands.

When I checked the letter my mother wrote after the prison visit my grandfather referred to, I found no mention of my father looking unwell. His poor appearance could not possibly have escaped her notice, but, wisely, she did not draw his attention to it. The lines my mother added to my grandfather's letter a day later are notable for their absence of disappointment and alarm when she had every reason to feel both:

14th May 1938

My dear Gottfried,

Aren't you surprised by Father coming to see us? I was and I must say he could not have done anything more sensible because family sentiments suffer if you don't see each other from time to time…Father related that your health isn't so good so please do everything in your power to remain strong

and well…everything's back on the beaten track again in my life. TG I feel fine and I don't have any other wishes, <u>other than just the one</u>. To come back to your health once again, please my darling, have a check-up. Above all your nerves are very frayed and something has to be done about them. I don't need to ask how your sleeping is. I know that old story from way back.

I assume, not knowing how long their request for a suspension of further imprisonment might take to be processed, and perhaps even doubting its success, my mother continued to send my father freshly laundered shirts.

…tomorrow my darling, your washing will go off. I'm only sending you shirts with attached collars because these are more convenient…keep being patient and imperturbable and don't lose courage.

Before she signed off, my mother assured her husband that my grandfather had *dealt splendidly* with all that he had requested in his previous letter and that *one does what one can.*

Her reference to medical check-ups was surprising, since I was not aware that they were still available to prisoners in Nazi jails in mid-1938, until Michael Viebig confirmed that prisoners were seen by a doctor every three months though hardly adequate for ailing inmates. Ironically, the one thing that would have restored my father's health was the very thing the authorities were threatening would now not take place, his release.

Initially, I was struck by the abruptness with which the letters from prison ended and those from concentration camp began. However, some explanations were already forthcoming in my father's first letter from Dachau, 5th June 1938.

Dachau 3K Concentration Camp

The following regulations must be observed in correspondence with prisoners:

1) Every protective custody prisoner may receive two letters or two cards a month from his relations and send the same to them. Letters to prisoners must be easily readable, written in ink, and can contain only 15 lines to a page. Only standard size notepaper is allowed. Envelopes must be unpadded. Only 5 x 12-pfennig stamps can be enclosed in a letter. Anything else is forbidden and will be subject to confiscation. Postcards can have 10 lines. Photographs cannot be used as postcards.

2) Cash remittances are allowed.

3) Newspapers are allowed but can only be ordered through the Dachau C.C. postal agency.

4) Packages may not be sent because prisoners can buy everything in the camp.

5) Petitions to the camp administration for release from protective custody are pointless.

All mail which fails to comply with these regulations will be returned to sender. If no sender is known, it will be destroyed.

The Camp Commander

My address:
Name: Gottfried Strauss
born on: 15 June 1907
Block: 4   Barrack: 1

____

(Stamp)
D.C.C. Office of Postal Censorship
Dachau 3 K, (date): 5 June 1938

My dearest little wife,

Today I first of all want to tell you about me, but before I do I want to say that I very much long for a sign of life from you.

I've been here since 28.V., and our community transport passed through Kulmbach where we spent a bit of time. So I was back in my original home once again. I'm so sorry to have worried you all about my health in my last letter from Halle. The Halle doctor was indeed right; he told me that the nervous manifestations would disappear when I get out of solitary confinement and have light and fresh air. I'm near the mountain range here and outside from morning to evening; as I've said, the doctor was right; so I would ask all of you dear ones as of today to stop worrying in the slightest about my health. I have the most enormous appetite and there's everything in the canteen here that the heart desires; and all you need is money; so please darling, every week send me 10 marks regularly, as regular as clockwork please, always on the same day. The maximum that I'm allowed to spend per week is 15 marks, but I do hope that I'll not only be able to manage with 10 marks a week but also will be able to improve my weight a little, which dropped in Halle. Did you [plural] receive my letter from Halle? I hope you and all of our dear ones are all right, because this time dear Father did not say anything; apparently you didn't know where I've landed up in the meanwhile. Let us all remain patient and steadfast, however long it takes till I'm with you again. As far as the settlement in the Kaufmann (patent) case is concerned, please notify Advocate Mälches that I reject it and ask for a judgment, because I do not know how long my custody will last. Incidentally, Dr. Mälches should write to me here and then I will correspond directly with him again. Now I want to send a few words to dear Father. Please, dear Irene, I ask you urgently to send the money immediately and never to forget to write my date of birth on the postal order and to leave the other side blank. With all my love, hugs and kisses.

How is dear Mother?   Your Gottfried

My dear Father, I was really very happy this time to get your lovely letter of 29.V. In future write to me again together with dear Irene on the same sheet as regular as clockwork. On 27.V. I was in the Kulmbach court prison for about five hours and was marched from the station through the streets. It was hard, but everything passes. Once again all my love and kisses for our relatives in Mülheim as well. Your Gottfried

My mother, grandfather and their families must have been enormously relieved when they received this letter, obviously not about my father being in concentration camp, but knowing he was alive. Their appeal to the authorities for a suspension of imprisonment and parole had failed which accounted for his arrival in Dachau. Subsequent research confirmed that on 27th May 1938, my father began his journey out of Halle and the next day became an inmate of Dachau concentration camp. Nine days after his arrival when he wrote his first letter, he still didn't know whether his loved ones knew of his fate.

Due to the strict censorship in these institutions of terror, my father's six letters and one postcard from concentration camp are devoid of any description of the immense suffering that was the lot of all prisoners. However, from first-hand accounts of fellow inmates like Paul Martin Neurath who wrote "The Society of Terror: Inside the Dachau and Buchenwald Concentration Camps," published by Paradigm Publishers, 2005, it was possible to enter the nightmare world that he, my father and thousands of other unfortunates endured.

Of the five rules and regulations stipulated by the camp commander and printed on official camp stationery–a four-sided, double-spaced leaflet–without a doubt the most disheartening concerned the futility of trying to get a prisoner released.

Until now, my father's imprisonment and sentencing seem to have been carried out in accordance with some corrupted form of German law. Based on this law, my mother and grandfather might have felt cautiously optimistic about appealing to the authorities for his release. However, with my father forced into concentration camp they would have realized they were dealing with a whole new order of things.

The tiny touches of humanity shown in Halle to my father, for example, my mother's letter from St. Marien hospital passed by the censor "in consideration of the illness," and my father's request to write a business letter in addition to writing to my mother, had possibly hoodwinked them into believing that the system in which they were caught up could still be counted on for some measure of decency and compassion. My father's unceremonious delivery to Dachau, however, surely put an end to all that!

I wonder about my father's thoughts on the way to Dachau. Did he still feel he was to blame for what had happened or was he starting to make connections between his trial and its verdict, his served sentence and his outrageous transfer to concentration camp?

When he got there he would have found himself amongst thousands of prisoners, including non-Jews, unjustly incarcerated for daring to hold political views inimical to those of National Socialism and, worse still, for being something other than pure Aryan. These included Jehovah's Witnesses, Catholic and Protestant priests, professional criminals and a-socials (a term the Nazis used to describe social misfits).

I don't know how my father was transported to Dachau. There was a difference in treatment of prisoners arriving in their hundreds and thousands on trains, and those arriving in much smaller groups by road; men arriving en mass by rail apparently suffered far worse abuse on the journey than those arriving in small trucks. My father's use of the word "station" would seem to indicate that he came by train, and yet his references to "community" transport and "Kulmbach court prison," together with the fact that prisoners who came from penitentiaries, prisons and court prisons were usually ferried in small trucks of no more than ten prisoners, would suggest he arrived by road. Then again, his journey may have combined both forms of travel.

In any event, the road travelers were guarded by regular police or prisoner personnel who generally did not manhandle or beat them. Up to the moment they left the van, the prisoners were in the hands of the civilian authorities even though legally they were recognized as prisoners of the Gestapo. Once they were handed over to the SS guards of the concentration camp "they [lost] their status as human beings and [became] something different." Eye-witness reports claim that all prisoners were received into Dachau and other camps in a similar fashion.

"Without any preparation they are faced with a completely new world, chased through an administrative procedure which, in spite of all the beating, works like clockwork."

"Guards swarm around the prisoners, striking, beating, shouting and kicking them and occasionally threatening them with a bullet…everybody gets beaten no matter what they do…after evening roll call, the newcomers are led to their barracks…during the night they recover to some degree, and in the morning it all looks like a bad dream…the prisoner's desire to keep his status as a man, and if need be to defend it, has not yet been entirely broken. But it has to be broken. Otherwise the administration could not keep thousands of prisoners together under conditions which, in ordinary prisons, would lead to riot and mutiny every day."

"Those in charge mistreat the newcomers systematically for several days. The prisoner, during hard labor, may faint over his wheelbarrow, topple over under the burden of heavy stones, collapse while being hit over the head with a club, but he will not be allowed to stay down. The officer's boot will bring him to life again…the initiation is over."

My father's phrase "It was hard" apparently referred to the humiliation of being marched like a convict through the familiar streets of his childhood. For obvious reasons he could not describe his "welcome" into the camp and I wondered, once he'd arrived, whether he still believed that his post-Halle existence would be an "improvement to [his] life, particularly if it is nothing but a staging post to [his] eventual freedom." In view of the fact that in 1938, not even most Nazis themselves knew what they would ultimately do with the Jews, my father's belief that protective custody and additional confinement (in a concentration camp) pending investigation were temporary measures is probably justifiable.

To read in my father's own words that he'd spent time in solitary confinement in Halle penitentiary, deprived of light and fresh air long enough to develop a skin disease which he referred to as "nervous manifestations," filled me with pity and rage. It was evidence from "the horse's mouth" that, indeed, he'd been subjected to grossly inhumane treatment. His loss of weight was probably due to a combination of severe depression, punitive denial of food and a meatless diet.

In any event, by the time he got to Dachau, my father was suffering semi-starvation which accounts for his desperate requests to my mother, twice in the space of a short letter, for money to buy food–the only way prisoners could supplement the minimal camp diet.

Interestingly, despite the lawless imprisonment, when postal orders arrived they were swiftly paid out to the prisoner in coins which they could spend in the canteen on butter, sugar, biscuits, canned fish, jams and molasses. My father needed to make up for his weight loss and boost himself for the long hours of hard labor he began as soon as he arrived in the camp. Extra rations were obtained from the canteen by two or three men from each barrack who were appointed to buy the food on behalf of dozens of their fellow prisoners which often led to mix-ups and an inequitable distribution of goods.

However, without financial assistance from my mother and grandfather, my father's daily diet would have been a breakfast of bread and a coffee flavored drink. Lunch was a quart of some thick stew of potatoes, peas or beans with meat or fish. In the evening there was "tea" (a sweet brew that the prisoners could not identify), with bread and either herring, cheese or sausages, and prunes with rice or porridge.

Apparently, the food "was sufficient in quantity and quality to keep a prisoner alive under the strain of hard labor." But staying alive did not mean keeping healthy, and it is a mark of the contempt in which the Nazi administration held prisoners that, for the "privilege" of being in a concentration camp and being horribly mistreated, they could add to the coffers of The Third Reich by contributing financially to their own well-being.

My father suggested a certain freedom in his letter when he wrote that he was able to spend his days in the fresh air in full view of the mountains surrounding Dachau. What he didn't report was that nature's scenery included heavily guarded walls and ditches, high voltage barbed wire and machine guns.

Nevertheless, his relief at having finally arrived in the place he'd been imagining and dreading for such a long time is probably genuine, since the macabre possibility had turned into a concrete reality against which he could now pitch himself.

In the summer when my father arrived at Dachau the day began at 3:20am and finished at 6:00pm. The prisoners went to work in any weather and worked alongside men who died from sunstroke. One prisoner gave evidence (his file on Dachau is kept at Yad Vashem) of men working in forty degrees heat, hatless, with shaven heads. If it rained they stood for hours in knee-deep water that gathered in gravel pits and in the winter men dropped dead from cold.

At 11:00am the men were marched back to the barracks for lunch, often being forced to sing along the way. Once there, they attended to things that could only be done during the noon break such as visiting the infirmary, the barbershop (contrary to my father's belief that in concentration camp his hair would have time to grow, a prisoner's hair had to be kept closely cropped as an intentional humiliation as well as a precaution against lice), the clothing department or the canteen for extra food, leaving little time to rest. At 12:30pm the whistle blew, the roll call was repeated (there were three a day) and the prisoners were marched back to work which consisted primarily of constructing the camp and the roads and military buildings around it.

Four days after he turned thirty-one my father wrote his second letter from Dachau in response to my mother's first of six he acknowledged receiving in concentration camp. Regrettably, none of hers survived:

Dachau, 19th June 1938

My beloved Treasure,

My joy over your most ardently longed-for letter was immense, and the same of course applies to receiving the postal order which I hereby confirm.

Since I have been here for 3 weeks already, I can give you the cheering news that I am fine, because the beginning was made somewhat difficult by the manual labor to which I am not accustomed; but I repeat once again it is quite impossible to compare things with my state of health in Halle. I have become used to the work, I have an appetite which is so enormous that I just cannot describe it to you. I look the way I did in March, 1935: tanned. Together we endure a cruel fate but I can adapt to any destiny and I have enough hard things behind me to be able to live in a state of habit. It is absolutely wonderful that you can support me, even though it adds up to a lot of money. Perhaps you'll write to dear Grandfather and ask him to make another transfer to you. I might occasionally just <u>once or twice</u> need 15 marks a week because I'd like to buy a number of implements. What is left over will improve my health and power of resistance. I'll write to Advocate Mälches this week directly. We're not going to pay another penny for fees and I agree with you about being fed up to the back teeth [with the patent]. By the way, I don't think it's very promising for dear Tutti and her husband to want to move to Kurt. I know the opposition doesn't come from Kurt, but I'm sure they have not made a happy choice as far as their new homeland is concerned. The matter can of course be pursued further though it is better for her to have 2 irons in the fire and to try and find another way. What do you think about this? Write to me about it and please send them my regards. Also my best regards to Mother, Father and Heinz. TG I don't do a lot of thinking about you, _my_ sweetheart, so that I won't be overcome by longing; can you grasp this? It's the most sensible thing. But sometimes it's really strong. Let's hope that fate will be kind to us. I was happy that you're fine and I feel so lucky that you're able to support me. Please send special greetings to my Father. He really mustn't spend any more money to try and get the procedure speeded up. Everything takes its time. Now I want to send you, my beloved Irene, all my love and kisses, in love your devoted Gottfried.

The "somewhat difficult" beginning my father refers to was, apparently, the physical work of digging gravel–one of the main jobs in Dachau–needed for almost everything; constructing roads, filling up excavations, making concrete walls, heat shafts, barracks and many other purposes. Paul Martin Neurath writes that the skin on the prisoners' hands and shoulders when they first arrived was tender and blisters formed and burst within a few hours, unaccustomed as they were to the pickaxe, shovel and wheelbarrow. Dust got into the open wounds which began to fester, developing large sores, often swelling to such an extent that they could no longer work, whereupon they dared to go to the infirmary where a few drops of iodine were applied and they were sent back to work. After a few minutes the wounds were dirty again. If one was lucky no serious infections developed.

I think of my father's soft-skinned hands and elegant, long fingers and wonder how much abuse they sustained.

The stone carriers suffered another kind of pain. The heavy concrete blocks they carried on their shoulders were jagged, with knife-sharp edges…which cut through their thin clothes and into the skin and flesh. If they tried to use their caps as cushions, they were beaten. The punishment was known as "twenty-five." The victim was strapped to a stand and given twenty-five heavy blows on the back and buttocks with a stick…sometimes a blanket was put over the victim's head to muffle his screams. In Dachau the "twenty-five" was usually combined with four days in the dungeon–a darkened cell–with one meal a day and was considered the heaviest of punishments. It was described as a place where "you are tortured beyond the limits of imagination."

I know from Noemi that my father was beaten in concentration camp. He dropped this fact randomly into a conversation he had with Noemi when she was in her late teens. Nearly twenty years had passed since the brutal beatings had occurred and still my father could not lay that nightmare to rest.

He added that in an attempt to stop the flogging, he learnt to play dead, which is truly remarkable since, according to the concentration camp literature, this did not usually prevent the attack from continuing until all twenty-five blows had been inflicted.

A family friend also told me my father had been subjected to water torture. She said that his head had been secured for a time (unspecified) under a slow dripping tap. Of all the varieties of torment and cruelty that concentration camp prisoners were subjected to, I had not read of this, though I had no grounds to doubt the veracity of the story; torturing defenseless prisoners gave vent to the guards' visceral hatred of the Jews, and others, and they seemed to thrive on inventing ever more "original" forms of punishment.

The men were also forbidden from complaining about their health, which probably accounts for my father's repeated assurances to my mother that he was fine. Sentimentality, "gushiness," or signs of moral strength or resistance were censored.

About two weeks after my father was transferred to Dachau, the Nazis arrested thousands of purportedly anti-social Jews, many of whom had been convicted for minor traffic violations, and threw them into Dachau, Sachsenhausen and Buchenwald concentration camps. As the number of prisoners swelled the overcrowding became oppressive. With them, the new arrivals brought information from the outside from which my father learnt that arrests were continuing in order to create ever more widespread panic amongst Jews to emigrate and also, perhaps, that America was imposing ever tighter immigration quotas which might explain his comment that the US as a refuge was now not a "happy choice for Tutti and her husband."

My father's use of the grammatical form of the third person, singular, as a ploy to discuss emigration seems to have slipped by the censor. In Dachau, prisoners were forbidden from corresponding on this subject, as the camp rules had stated, or request or receive information about steps their relatives might be taking to secure their release, however, the number of ruses employed by prisoners to get information through in either direction was legion.

Following these mass arrests, proof of intention to leave Germany, such as the possession of ship tickets, and financial means, became the pathway to freedom, sometimes after only a few days or weeks in the camp.

Though my father seemed convinced his delay in exiting Dachau was related to his contractual obligation (most likely his bond), his release depended as much on my mother's efforts to run the "bureaucratic gauntlet" as it did on any systematic Nazi plan to release prisoners.

Could my father have truly believed by then that his "contractual obligation" was worth the paper it was written on?

In July, he was moved from Barrack 1 into Barrack 3 with no explanation.

Dachau, 3rd July 1938

My beloved sweetheart,

I was delighted to receive your lovely letter, as always; and the same goes for the letter from Father. I am decidedly well; that's what you want to know above all else.

I was very pleasantly surprised to receive 10 marks each from you and Father at the same time; that obviously will take care of two weeks, and I'll be able to manage a treat. I think my darling that you misunderstood me in my last letter; I said that I might need a total of 15 marks once or twice but not every month. But this isn't needed anymore either because I'm now managing fine with 10 marks, since my appetite has returned to normal; I look well. The amount of 40 marks a month isn't a trifle apart from the other financial sacrifices that you've had to make up to now. I know how hard all of this is. Haven't you written to Grandfather on my behalf? I was very happy to hear that Father has put new products into his business; the right thing would be to stock textiles as well. <u>How is dear Tutti? I do hope that the huge doctor's bills are coming to an end. I gathered with interest from your letter that she wants to immigrate to Columbia with her husband. It was right for her not to want to go to Kurt because the difficulties are so immense that all efforts are pointless</u>. And what will happen to us? Wait and see, hope and have patience. Please write whether you or Father received my letter which I wrote in May from Halle police headquarters.

You haven't confirmed receipt of it despite its contents being important, although in the meantime they've been superceded. I am now waiting for information from you because you've written to me that in your next letter you want to be more detailed. I had mail from Mälches again. On 6 July, yet another new application from Mrs. Kaufmann is expected. I'm writing to him that if any decisions have to be made he should contact you because you are familiar with my point of view and you have power of attorney. I am relieved if we don't have to have any more business dealings with Mrs. Kaufmann and will be able to get a bit of money for the project. How are Mother and all the dear relatives? Are you enjoying yourself at work with the "old girl," your boss's delightful sister? I will close now once again. All my love and kisses from your Gottfried who loves you deeply.

Warmest regards to all the dear ones.

Despite the Nazi's explicit policy of wanting to cleanse Germany of its Jews, any discussion of emigration in Dachau was a forbidden and therefore risky business. The camp administration there wanted to be solely responsible for those it released and for those it wouldn't. Hence my father's second try to disguise his references to the topic was underlined in dark pink pencil by the censor. Nonetheless, the letter reached my mother intact.

The next letter in the collection is the fourth and last from Dachau in the four months my father was interned there.

Dachau, 28th August 1938

My truly adored Irene,

I received your letter with great pleasure and today I want to reply in somewhat more detail than last time. Above all I can tell you that given the circumstances I am still uniformly fine. I thank you warmly for the remittances and wonder whether things can remain this way later as well; but given time, things will become clearer. I was delighted to hear that Father, in addition to dear Fred and Tutti, is fine. And you my treasure? It would be desirable for you not to spend unnecessary money on things that aren't urgent; but obviously it's quite right never to interrupt the treatment

until you are fully recovered. How long do you
think you can carry on working? It seems to me
very short-sighted that Eric is still here with
little Klara. As far as Heinz is concerned it is
perhaps necessary for him to stay because of your
dear parents although this may be quite wrong.
I've also been thinking, my darling, whether you
should wait for me or whether you yourself should
try and find a way of keeping body and soul together
somewhere else. Though this isn't absolutely
necessary since I assume you will continue to be
able to survive here, but there is something to
be said for leaving. The situation is different
for dear Fred who is still under a contractual
obligation. If he stays in Germany, despite his
mediocre livelihood his dear wife would have to
make sure that he agrees to go overseas with her
in order to establish an agricultural livelihood.
Perhaps...[rest of page missing...]

South America where land for cultivation is being made available. Perhaps later, once I'm free
again, we could also leave and settle there. If
Fred or Tutti were to make representation to the
boss, probably this would be more successful than
the previous correspondence. And now something
about the payment of the patent fees! I have [...]
Mr. Stern through a business partner of...please
immediately [rest of page missing...]

By now, the censor no longer bothered with his pink pencil and
instead, roughly cut off half of the third and fourth pages. Trying to
make sense of my father's thoughts about emigration with sections
of the letter missing proved difficult enough without attempting

to follow his prevarications. Yet his suggestions and counter-suggestions bear witness to the fear and confusion for every Jew aware of the urgency to flee and the difficulties entailed therein. What my father's "contractual obligation" was all about was a total mystery, since a prisoner on a bond was usually freed to enjoy it whereas my father went directly from Halle into concentration camp. However, his well-meant criticism of his brother-in-law, Eric, and his wife not yet having left Germany, was unequivocal and may have come from information he'd picked up in the camp.

With good reason, money worries continued to plague him. His bank account was blocked (and perhaps he now understood it would remain so) and he knew that a shortage of currency could come to mean the difference between life and death.

Whether my mother was still being treated for the same illness as before is unexplained. My father's question about how long she could go on working may have alluded to her health, or to the real possibility that her Jewish boss's business was slated to be taken over by the Nazis.

The next letter in the collection comes from Buchenwald.

It's possible my father's latest change of location was due to the evacuation and expansion of Dachau some time in late September 1938, in preparation for the planned seizure of yet more Jews. Research showed that my father arrived in Buchenwald on 22nd September 1938.

What astonished me most was my father's undisguised references to emigration, a subject that wiped all other items off the agenda; although the letter bears the censor's stamp there was no attempt to tear off, underline or cross out anything. I believed this to be an oversight on the part of camp censorship until I read that prisoners in Buchenwald, unlike those in Dachau, were actually told to correspond with their relatives about the previously taboo subject of emigration. There were, however, guidelines.

Buchenwald stationery varied only slightly from that of Dachau.

Letter will not be despatched unless block no. is given

Write only on the ruled lines!

(Stamp) Cash remittances are only permitted by postal order

Weimar-Buchenwald
Concentration Camp
Extract from the Camp Regulations:

Every prisoner is allowed to receive and send 2 letters or 2 postcards a month. The lines in the letter must be clear and legible. Mailings which do not comply with these requirements will not be forwarded. Irrespective of their contents, packages cannot be received. Cash remittances are allowed; everything can be bought in the camp. National Socialist newspapers are allowed, but must be ordered by the prisoner in person via the concentration camp postal agency.

The Camp Commander

My exact address:

Protective custody prisoner
Gottfried Strauss
No. 8863
Block: 9
Weimar-Buchenwald
Concentration Camp

(Stamp) Letters which are confusing and difficult to read cannot be censored and will be destroyed.

Release dates cannot yet be indicated. Visits to the camp are prohibited. Queries are pointless.

My beloved Irene,

I have received your lovely letters, for which I longed so greatly, of 4.10 and 11.10, as well as the lines from Father and both your remittances; heartfelt thanks for everything. You don't need to be quite so brief, my dear lass; I'm interested in particular in knowing whether the emigration matter is working out. Should it prove necessary for you to have a picture of me in order for the exit papers, e.g. passport, to be completed, I can get one to you, as well as a doctor's certificate which can be issued here at my request by the camp doctor. Please tell me if you need both of these. As far as I am concerned, I would emigrate to any country in the world, but I think that with an eye to a possible release the USA or Mexico are not as favourable as for example Shanghai in China or Abyssinia and other similar countries. The main thing, of course, is that at least the papers get drawn up for some country or other abroad and that these be submitted in duplicate to the authorities, not disregarding Halle. It is probably also important to produce a steamer ticket; naturally in such a case, this would have to be cashed in again by the travel bureau in the case of failure. I do not despair because you, my precious lass, will leave no stone unturned. However, if this or that step depends on the lack of the necessary financial resources, then I would ask you, notwithstanding your normal pride, to ask all our relatives for help and support. The right thing would be for you and dear Father to declare yourselves willing to emigrate together with me and of course to also submit the papers for this. The fact that dear Heinz and Eric excluded themselves is something I wanted in their interest. I myself am remaining strong and patient; given the circumstances I am fine. With profound love and longing, Your Gottfried

Space for Censorship Stamp:	Block Head Approval:
(stamp)	
BCC Postal Agency	
Censored: (initials)	

Conditions in Buchenwald were appalling and very different from those in Dachau though there was no less terror. Cleanliness and order were replaced by dirt and disorganization and a great deal of bribery and racketeering was conducted by the prisoners.

Whereas Dachau stood on gravel, a relatively clean material, Buchenwald was built on clay which smeared and stuck to everything. With an accompanying water shortage, prisoners could not wash their hands or keep their clothing clean, and were punished for appearing dirty at roll-call. Lack of water also affected health and hygiene and made taking care of wounds impossible, sometimes resulting in blood poisoning. Furthermore, while Dachau was free of vermin, barracks in Buchenwald were occasionally lice infected.

The greater number of hours of work and the slower tempo could exhaust a man as thoroughly as the terrific speed with which prisoners were chased in Dachau, especially as the food was so much worse and the men could not quench their thirst. Moreover, whereas Dachau was situated on level ground, Buchenwald was built on a steep mountain, making the transportation of great masses of material more strenuous.

In Dachau, all food and tobacco found in a prisoner's possession during working hours was considered contraband and frequently led to punishment. In Buchenwald, every prisoner had a bread bag in which he carried his noon rations so only a large quantity of food and tobacco aroused suspicion. With the help of this bread bag, a tremendous amount of smuggling and trading went on all over the area, and the administration was practically powerless to stop it since it was impossible to search ten thousand bread bags a day.

The fact that my father's first letter from Buchenwald is almost entirely devoted to the subject of emigration lends weight to the probability that he wrote it after Kristallnacht which had raged throughout the entire country during the night of 9th-10th November (my mother's 27th birthday was the 10th), and marked a turning point in the Nazis' determination to get rid of the Jews.

About two weeks before "The Night of the Shattered Glass," Hitler had ordered the deportation of seventeen thousand Polish Jews, many of them resident in Germany for generations, to the Polish border. Poland denied them entry so they were abandoned, caught between the two borders in the cold and without food and shelter. Officials had moved them without warning, allowing them to pack only a few necessities. As the pitiable Jews languished between two countries in the freezing wet, no-man's-land, a young Polish Jew living in Paris, Herschel Grynszpan, whose parents and sister were among the deportees, was driven to despair. He shot and killed Ernst vom Rath, a diplomat from the German embassy in Paris. The Nazis used the death of vom Rath as a convenient excuse to launch Kristallnacht, the worst pogrom Germany had seen.

For an account of how the news of this unprecedented demonstration of anti-Semitic terror was received in Buchenwald, I will again quote Paul Martin Neurath who arrived there from Dachau two days after my father.

"Rumours quickly spread…that an attempt had been made on Hitler's life and terror struck the camp…The Jews were certain that they would all be shot. Soon the truth came out that a young Polish Jew had shot a German attaché in Paris which sounded less ominous. However, the next day it began. Jews were brought into the camp in their thousands, in all stages of life–wounded, sick, crippled, with broken limbs, missing eyes, fractured skulls, half dead and dead."

"For a while nothing happened to the Jews…but then the discrimination and deprivation began. First, every Jew had to send home a mimeographed slip, announcing, 'Until further notice I am under mail blockade and therefore am not permitted to receive or mail letters, cards or parcels. Inquiries to the administration are forbidden and will prolong the ban on writing.'

"Next the Jews' food ration was cut and every third Sunday became a fast day. After Kristallnacht, a loaf of bread ordinarily given to two men now had to do for five. Margarine was cut out. The allowance of cheese and sausage was cut in half. The soup portions were decreased. Smoking was forbidden. No money [from relatives] was handed out. Finally, the Jews were excluded from medical treatment, both clinical and in the infirmary. A Jew had shot a German. The guilty had to pay for it."

"Mercifully, the non-Jewish political prisoners came to the rescue. Camp food and medical supplies were smuggled both to the pogrom Jews and to Jews in the camp."

"It was the heroic time of Buchenwald when ragged, emaciated, hungry and exhausted prisoners fought the battle for the lives of nearly ten thousand of their Jewish fellow prisoners who had been brought into the camp after Kristallnacht."

Nonetheless, despite the claimed heroism, more than a thousand Jews died in concentration camps that night and ninety-one others died in cities around Germany during the first twenty-four hours of violence. In Buchenwald, an estimated three hundred and fifty Jews died that winter.

Seeing the results of the savagery inflicted on the Jews during Kristallnacht undoubtedly added to my father's desperation to immigrate to any country in the world, including such far-flung places as South America, Africa and China.

On 15th October 1938, the German authorities had announced that the passports of all German Jews were cancelled and new papers had to be acquired. This, obviously, was my mother's job, that exhausting and frustrating process of having to wait in long lines in over-crowded embassies and travel agencies dealing with many thousands of applications from frantic Jews.

These new papers were official documents that had to be presented to the Gestapo in duplicate to get their permission to leave and in my father's case, also to Halle prison authorities.

Mercifully, in all the calamities that had befallen my parents, my father was spared the direct brutality of Kristallnacht.

If he sent my mother a notice about a mail blockade–that lasted about two months–she did not keep it with the other camp letters. Nevertheless, my father refers to the clamp down in his 4th December 1938 letter. The censor had returned to do his mischief–though not on the subject of emigration–roughly tearing at the letter and making page one and two incomprehensible. The remaining words sound grim, and my father has reconsidered the US as an option for my mother. The long-awaited affidavit had arrived from my father's US cousin, Kurt.

Buchenwald, 4th December 1938

My beloved Irene,

After a lengthy interval today you are again to have the pleasure of hearing from me in somewhat more detail. How are you and how are all our dear ones? The thought that all of you are presumably not doing well, worries me.

What I can tell you about myself, my dear lass is the fact that as far as my health is concerned I'm still fine. Bearing our fate is equally hard for all of us today. Your last letters which I have received were dated 4.10 and 11 October. Should you have informed me since then of any important things, please repeat them. The fact that I haven't had any post from you for so long is probably because an October letter

[illegible] since it is the 3rd distributed, then postal services were suspended. The last cash remittances are dated 5.11 for 5 and 10 marks. That will now come to an end. But perhaps it is possible to obtain modest on-going support from one of our many American relatives. I am more worried, however, about how you and our loved ones are going to keep body and soul together. Another problem is how the emigration is to be financed. I don't want to think that for lack of travel funds things will collapse at the moment when I receive permission to emigrate. In any case, I advise you, and now regret that it didn't happen six months ago, to enquire of Kurt about the possibility of finding a livelihood with him or somewhere else in the world from where, later, you could help me better than you could from here. I'm sure this will be the case. Incidentally, it might be a good idea not only to maintain the USA affidavit, but to look at immigrating to a colonial area. With my undying love, Your Gottfried.

It is somewhat unnerving to read that my father believed my mother could more effectively work towards securing his release from outside Germany. Had she left Germany without him, my father surely would have perished. What he didn't know and what she wouldn't divulge was that she was using her feminine wiles to persuade the Nazis to grant her husband his freedom. Her cousin Meir, from Essen, who escaped to Israel in 1939, remembers that my mother dyed her hair blonde in order to appear more Aryan to her Nazi interlocutors. Meir relates how his father was on excellent terms with the Gestapo Chief of Police in Essen. The two men had fought together in WWI and remained friendly after the war. He described the Police Chief as an "unwilling" Nazi who not only warned his father about Kristallnacht and offered his home as a place for the family to hide, but also helped my mother navigate her way through the Gestapo bureaucracy while she was working towards having my father released from Buchenwald.

Buchenwald, 19th January 1939

My dear Irene, I hope these lines find you well and also all our dear ones. Given the circumstances I am fine and I profoundly hope that the words in your last letter will soon turn out to be true. Please don't write more than 2 letters a month. Just in case, my farewell greetings to Eric and Heinz. How is my dear Father? In my thoughts I tell you of my great love and embrace you. My warmest kisses, your Gottfried.

The first real hint that my father's freedom was within reach comes from the words "…and I profoundly hope that the words in your last letter will soon turn out to be true…" and in an undated postcard which seems to have been written some time after 19th January he writes that his "indescribable joy" went hand-in-hand with a foreboding about my grandfather's well-being and was an omen of unimaginable things to come.

Buchenwald

My sweetheart, the purpose of this card is to ask you to send me the money for the trip which must be at hand here in case of a release. I received the cash remittance from Kulmbach and from you, my darling, as well as your letter of 14.12. My joy was indescribable, although I strongly suspect you are keeping me in the dark about my Father. How is dear Fred? Will he definitely manage to wind up the business aspects by the relevant deadline? Regards to all our nearest and dearest, lots of kisses, Your Gottfried.

Against incredible odds, in ways which can never be fully or accurately described, my mother had indeed left "no stone unturned" and my father was, at long last, to be released. However, his joy was diluted by the absence of news about my grandfather.

My father's final communication after his three years and two months incarceration was a telegram dispatched from Halle at 16:55 on 22nd January 1939, where he had stopped off on his way from Buchenwald to Mülheim. It appears from what he had written in an earlier letter that, since his transfer from jail to Dachau had been organised from Halle, his release from Buchenwald had to be authorized by the Halle administration. Three days after my father's expressed hope that what my mother had written would soon come to pass, did so.

HAPPILY UNDERWAY ARRIVAL TIME UNCERTAIN
IF POSSIBLE TELEGRAM FATHER FAREWELL
GREETINGS GOTTFRIED

MEMENTOS

Parents Irene and Gottfried Strauss on their wedding day, December 1, 1935.

Karl Strauss sometime in middle age.

Maternal grandmother, Johanna Meyer (nee Strauss).

Paternal grandmother, Frieda Strauss (nee Hamburger).

Mother, Irene Meyer at 19.

Newspaper photo of Ida Weber with my grandfather's
name on her placard, November, 1938.

Paternal grandfather, Karl Strauss with fellow WWI soldiers.
Back row, second from left.

Halle Prison at the time of my father's incarceration.

My father's seventeen-page, hand-written plea to The People's Court in Berlin.

Konzentrationslager Dachau 3 K

Folgende Anordnungen sind beim Schriftverkehr mit Gefangenen zu beachten:

1.) Jeder Schutzhaftgefangene darf im Monat zwei Briefe oder zwei Karten von seinen Angehörigen empfangen und an sie absenden. Die Briefe an die Gefangenen müssen gut lesbar mit Tinte geschrieben sein und dürfen nur 15 Zeilen auf einer Seite enthalten. Gestattet ist nur ein Briefbogen normaler Größe Briefumschläge müssen ungefüttert sein. In einem Briefe dürfen nur 5 Briefmarken à 12 Pfg. beigelegt werden. Alles andere ist verboten und unterliegt der Beschlagnahme. Postkarten haben 10 Zeilen. Lichtbilder dürfen als Postkarten nicht verwendet werden.

2.) Geldsendungen sind gestattet.

3.) Zeitungen sind gestattet, dürfen aber nur durch die Poststelle des K. L. Dachau bestellt werden.

4.) Pakete dürfen nicht geschickt werden, da die Gefangenen im Lager alles kaufen können.

5.) Entlassungsgesuche aus der Schutzhaft an die Lagerleitung sind zwecklos.

Alle Post, die diesen Anforderungen nicht entspricht, geht an die Absender zurück. Ist kein Absender bekannt, so wird sie vernichtet.

Der Lagerkommandant.

Absender:

Meine Anschrift:

Name: Gottfried Strauß

geboren am: 15. Juni 1907

Block: 4   Stube: 1

Postzensurstelle K. L. D.

Dachau 3 K, den: 5. Juni 1938

Mein liebes Fräuchen!

Heute will ich zuerst von mir erzählen, aber doch noch vorher einfügen, daß ich mich sehr nach einem Lebenszeichen von Dir sehne. Also seit 28. V. bin ich hier und zwar hatten wir auf dem Gemeinschafts-Transport auch Kulmbach berührt und Aufenthalt. So war ich einmal wieder in der Ur-Heimat. Ich bereue, daß ich Euch in meinem letzten Brief aus Halle bezüglich meiner Gesundheit beunruhigt habe. Tatsächlich hatte der Hallische Arzt recht; er sagte mir, daß

My father's first letter to my mother from Dachau concentration camp, June 5, 1938.

037 Telegramm   **Deutsche Reichspost**

37 HALLESAALE /1 14 22 1625 =

STRAUSZ BACHSTR 62 MUELHEIMRUHR =

Amt Mülheim (Ruhr)

GLUECKLICH UNTERWEGS ANKUNFTSZEIT UNGEWISS MOEGLICHST

VATER TELEGRAFISCH ABSCHIED BESTELLEN = GOTTFRIED + +

Telegram sent by my father announcing his release
from Buchenwald concentration camp.

Pol. Nr.8863, S t r a u s s, Gottfried
Jude

15.6.07.Kulmbach-B.
Kaufmann
23 Sep. 1938

Mülheim-Ruhr

entlassen 22.1.39

Document showing my father's arrival at Buchenwald,
September 23, 1938, with "released" hand-written.

Konzentrations-Lager Buchenwald

Familienname: S t r a u s s,	Pol Häftling Nr. 8863
Vorname: Gottfried	Jude Block:
geb. am 15.6.07 in Kulmbach – B.	Schutzhaft angeordnet:
Beruf: Kaufmann	am: 11.5.38 durch (Behörde): Gestapo Halle
Religion: mos. Staat: D.R.	Bisherige Parteizugehörigkeit: keine
verh., led., gesch. Frau: Irene St. Mülheim –R. Bachstr. 62	Vorstrafen: 2, Devisenverbrechen, Vorbereitung zum Hochverrat 2 J.3 M. Z. , 3 Jahre Ehrverlust

Grund: nach verbüsster Strafe wegen Vorb.z.Hochverrat. (Begleitung eines illeg. Funktionärs der SPD).	in Dachau 27.5.38 eingeliefert: von D. 23.9.38
	entlassen: 22.1.39.
I.T.S. FOTO No 009658	überführt:
	zurück:
	(Lichtbild)

Release form from Buchenwald listing the charges against my father,
"Preparation for high treason and three years loss of civil rights."

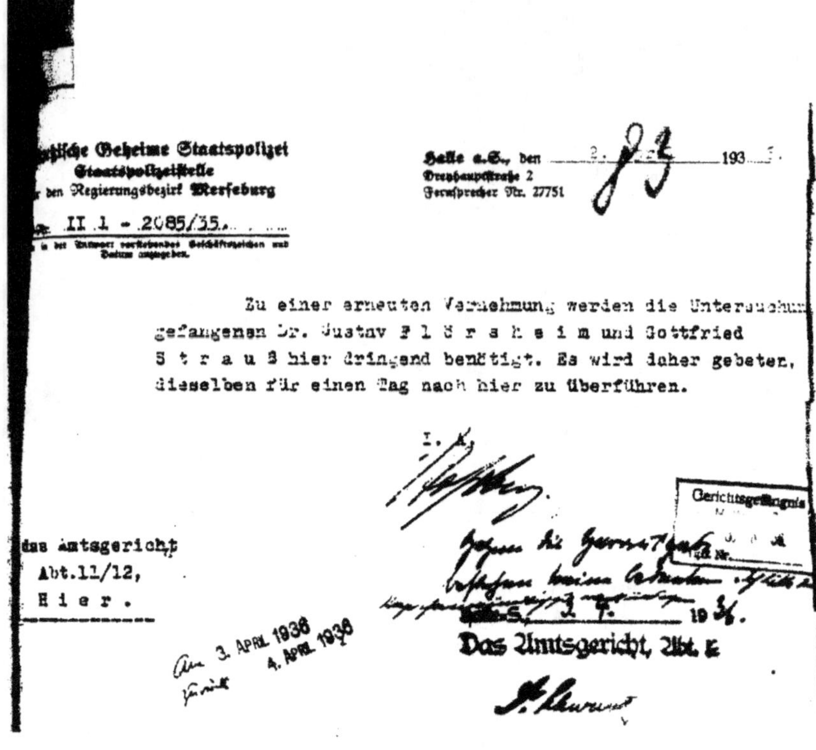

Geheime Staatspolizei
Staatspolizeistelle
für den Regierungsbezirk Merseburg

Halle a.S., den 2. 193
Dreyhauptstraße 2
Fernsprecher Nr. 27751

II 1 - 2085/35.

Zu einer erneuten Vernehmung werden die Untersuchungs-
gefangenen Dr. Gustav Flörsheim und Gottfried
Strauß hier dringend benötigt. Es wird daher gebeten,
dieselben für einen Tag nach hier zu überführen.

das Amtsgericht
Abt.11/12,
Hier.

Das Amtsgericht, Abt.

To the SS (Gestapo)

2nd April, 1936

We urgently need the arrested prisoners Dr. Gustav Floersheim and Gottfried Strauss to be brought here for a day for a renewed interrogation.

Signed

Magistrates Court.

Copy of a letter from the Halle Magistrate's Court calling for my father's, and his uncle's, re-interrogation April 2, 1936.

My parents in their thirties.

With sister, Noemi Dalidakis, at the Federal Archives in Berlin, 2003.

With Noemi (left) on my 70th birthday.

Gottfried and Irene in late middle age.

My father was no longer a prisoner of the Nazis though I hesitate to describe him as a free man; he carried the emotional and psychological scars of his ordeal all his life. Nevertheless, he and my mother were preparing to head for Shanghai, the only city in the world where, in 1939, no documents or visas of any kind were required. My grandfather would not be accompanying them. Although my mother had finally received an affidavit from the US–my father referred to it in his 4th December letter from Buchenwald–it would have come with an immigration number and would-be émigrés had to wait to be called by the US government. My parents couldn't or didn't want to wait. Noemi and I believed that the Gestapo had given them forty-eight hours to leave Germany, but the date on a postcard Noemi found from my uncle Heinz welcoming my parents to Hong Kong after four weeks at sea seems to indicate they were given a month.

Additional travel documents my mother might have secured for other countries may also have been pending when my father was released from concentration camp, but my parents favored the immediate accessibility of Shanghai.

Though the next decade of my parents' lives was not without its considerable hardships they were free from Nazi persecution and were able to leave Germany and join my two uncles in Shanghai in March 1939. My paternal grandfather was not so lucky. Apart from guesswork about his arrest during Kristallnacht, the only reliable snippet of information about his fate after my parents' departure arrived from an unexpected source.

Early in 1991 when I was forty-seven and still living in Melbourne, I had come across an article in an Australian newspaper which described the work of the International Tracing Service, a body which, at the end of World War II, began searching for people who had become displaced during the war or had gone missing altogether. By the early Nineties, the ITS's work included the gathering and classifying of records of people who had spent time in concentration camps and prisons, Jews who had been deported to death camps and other categories of people whose fate was unknown to their families. Based in Bad Arolsen, Germany, with branches all over the world, the article reported that the ITS was inviting enquiries from interested bodies or individuals though it warned that its files were not yet computerized and enquiries could take a long time to process. Noemi and I agreed I should write to enquire about what had become of our grandfather in the years after my parents left Germany. We did not tell our mother since there was no reason to believe that after so many years of refusing to speak about the past she'd suddenly cooperate and besides, she was already exhibiting signs of early dementia. She did, however, supply my grandfather's date and place of birth and my paternal grandmother's maiden name, which I included in my letter.

Every few months thereafter I received a standard letter informing me that, as yet, nothing had been found.

Then, in March 2000, nine years after my initial approach, I received a letter dated October 1996 consisting of five lines about my grandfather's fate:

STRAUSS, Karl, born in Hollfeld on 5.5.1873,

was interned in the police prison of Frankfurt

Main from 30th April, 1943 to 10th May, 1943.

Transported to Concentration Camp Auschwitz.

Why the letter had taken four years to reach me is a mystery. I had waited almost a decade to learn the whereabouts of my grandfather during the final days of his life. When I called Noemi to tell her the ghastly news that our grandfather had perished in Auschwitz she completely surprised me. She already knew and thought I did, too. She had been hoping for more information about the years before his terrible end.

I suppose I should have assumed that my grandfather was murdered in an extermination camp in Europe, the way thousands of other Jews were, but in 1991 I hadn't allowed myself to think along those lines because it was easier not to. However, after working with my parents' letters I was ready to face our family's difficult history. There were still about four years of my grandfather's life during the war I knew nothing about and I wondered if I ever would.

In 2003, in a further unexpected discovery, Noemi came across another letter while she was clearing out drawers in my mother's flat. It had not been kept as part of my parents' correspondence. This one was dated 19th May 1940, and was written from Amberg penitentiary located in south-eastern Germany. It was from my grandfather to my father and one marvels that it reached Shanghai during the war, since judging from the dates mentioned, letters from Shanghai to Germany took between four and five weeks.

Once the letter was deciphered and translated from Gothic German, I understood that my grandfather and father were still in contact fifteen months after my parents had emigrated. I wondered whether these were months of hope in which both parties still believed in an eventual reunion, despite the war and the long stretches of waiting for news.

The two-sided brownish leaflet is similar to my father's letters from concentration camp with a plethora of rules, prohibitions and visiting times listed on the upper third of the first page.

For ease of comprehension, I have edited the letter:

My dear children, I received your letter of 3.III on 9.IV and your letter 1.IV on 2.V. I'm very happy to know that you are all well and managing financially... obviously all things considered I can also report on a satisfactory situation. On 10.IV it was a year since I arrived here, but it is still too early to be transferred to level two or three, for that I will have to wait till the autumn. I am really delighted that Irene's dear parents arrived safely and I can vividly imagine the joyful reunion...Siegfried Sündemann...and family are in Montevideo and they're doing well. But their parents are still in Bayreuth. The dear ones in Wilme-R. sent me a letter a while ago and I was also happy that they're all well and a few days ago I received a postcard from uncle Sigmund about my things which are with Nathan in Kulmbach: I am supposed to have them sent on to Nüremberg and now I'm going to see whether I can get permission to visit Uncle Jacob and see to some more matters. Uncle Sigmund wrote to me that now he wants to seriously investigate the Aryan matter a clarification of which would naturally be of great interest to me. For your good wishes on my birthday, thank you so much and I reciprocate, dear Gottfried on yours too, wishing you very many happy returns of the day although these lines will reach you a little late. May your undertakings continue to be crowned with success and may the Good Lord see to it that everything you and yours wish for themselves comes true since your well-being is of special comfort to me and I can assure you time and again that in my faith in God I shall follow your advice and not lose courage. The man in the bunk next to me is called Loewenstein from Nüremberg whose son is going to immigrate to Shanghai in June and probably will meet you there.

To our dear ones in the U.S.A., please in the meanwhile send regards from me.

In a short while I may perhaps be given permission to write directly. I'm now reading a book called "Asia 38" with a lot of pictures including the Bund...and tea houses in Chinatown. It contains lots of details about farming industry and also about customs and traditions. Reading it helps me to pass the time more quickly.

In order to receive your return letter as soon as possible I remain with heartfelt greetings and kisses

Your loving Father

Heartfelt greetings to the parents, Eric and Heinz

The Amberg letter tore at my heart, and does every time I read it, causing me immense sorrow. I now knew that its sixty-seven year old author had become trapped in a Nazi jail. He had done everything in his power to help his incarcerated son only to become ensnared himself for reasons which would eventually become clear. And yet his uncomplaining words project faith and hope and an altruism and generosity of spirit.

Siegfried Sündermann was a name completely unknown to me and yet, since my grandfather had unwittingly supplied a first and second name, and a place, I felt compelled to look for this total stranger, beginning my search on the web for the address of the Jewish Community in Montevideo. By chance, as I was about to write to the Community, my husband received an invitation to give a lecture there, and was able to make enquiries on my behalf. I was delighted when he returned to Israel with the New York address of Sündermann's son, Julio, whom I subsequently contacted. Julio wrote back that his father had died fifteen years earlier and he himself had not heard him speak of my grandfather, but he thought a cousin in Montevideo might know more. Unfortunately, my letter to the cousin was never answered which brought the investigation to an end. Months later, while examining research found about my grandfather, I learned that he'd stated during a police interrogation that Sündermann was his cousin.

My grandfather's mention of seeking permission to visit an "Uncle Jacob," also unknown to me, was puzzling until it suddenly struck me that Jacob was probably in another part of the prison, since allowing prisoners out to visit relatives was unheard of during the Nazi years.

My grandfather's reference to his only sibling, Sigmund, and the "Aryan matter," triggered the memory of a conversation my parents had with Sigmund's sons while they and I were visiting New York in 1971, long after Sigmund had died. At the time I was in my late twenties and too self-absorbed to pay attention to things which seemed not to concern me, that is, "the Aryan matter" and regrettably, I don't recall what was said.

As I was rifling through some documents Noemi sent me at the very beginning of my research which I'd forgotten I had, I discovered two letters that Sigmund had written from the US to my parents in Shanghai, shortly after the outbreak of the war. In the first dated 5th October 1939 Sigmund wrote, "…we haven't received any mail from Karl for five weeks…everything has broken down because of the war…we are really worried."

Sigmund was also anxious about the fate of his brother in a second letter written eighteen months later:

6th March 1941

White Plains

N.Y.

The war, dear Gottfried, will continue for a longer time than we thought. The criminal is still strong and we must do something for your dear father during this year.

Three years were still missing in my grandfather's life, from the time of the Amberg letter to the time of his transportation to Auschwitz. With that gap and the many unanswered questions raised by my parents' letters, it felt timely to visit Yad Vashem, Jerusalem's Holocaust Memorial where a friend and former lecturer in Holocaust Studies, Yaacov Lozowick, was then Director of Archives. After I gave him a thumbnail sketch of the events covered in the letters, and a few details about my grandfather, he suggested that German archives would yield more information.

As it happened, Yaacov had recently been in contact with a group of professional German researchers in Berlin who comb archives all over the country for the sort of historical material I was looking for. He assured me the group's knowledge of English would make communication easy, and if I believed the task too onerous to undertake myself, the German scholars, who represent an organization called Facts and Files, would most likely be able to help me.

Following Yaacov's good counsel, I prepared a document with information from the letters and included the names, dates and places of birth of my parents, my maternal grandparents, my paternal grandfather and his wife's maiden name.

I attached a copy of my father's letter to the Halle magistrate of 10th August 1936, and devised a list of key questions: was my father arrested because of his connection to his uncle and his uncle's friend, both of whom were, apparently, political opponents of the Nazis? What evidence was brought against him? What were the charges? Why did he have to serve a six-month sentence even before his main hearing? Was there any information about the abortion performed on my mother and/or her mystery illness? I also included the few facts I had about my grandfather but asked that priority be given to researching my parents.

Two months passed before a thick "Deutsche Post" envelope arrived from Facts and Files. Inside was a twenty-six page document, in German, with a brief cover letter in English explaining that the material titled "Bill of Indictment" 28th September 1936 had come from the Federal Archives in Berlin, and was the first of several files concerning my father that they had extracted. They promised there were more to come.

With the help of an excellent computer translation program I began work on the document while wondering whether I'd ever be able to manage. My parents' letters were written in everyday conversational German. This official document, however, used a more formal German suitable for legal matters. I had forgotten that it is not uncommon for German words to be made up of twenty-six or more letters. Thankfully, the longer I applied myself to the job the better at it I became.

Addressed to the Fifth Criminal Division of the Supreme Court in Berlin, the Bill of Indictment describes in considerable detail the background to the events and people my father had mentioned in his letter to the Halle magistrate.

According to the Indictment, Franz Krause, the gentleman my father and his uncle Dr. Gustav Flörsheim went to see in Tetschen, Czechoslovakia, in November 1935, had been a prominent member of the Social Democratic Party at the time of Hitler's rise to power. After the Führer abolished the party in 1933 and arrested many of its top officials, Krause and others, fearing for their lives, fled to Czechoslovakia where they went underground and continued to work towards their goal of overthrowing the Nazis. However, in order to function efficiently and to keep the SPD updated, the party needed to maintain an army of sympathizers in Germany, some of whom would travel back and forth and pass on information about political, economic and social developments in The Third Reich.

After his flight, Franz Krause maintained a close relationship with Dr. Gustav Flörsheim who happened to be hosting his friend on a day in October 1934 when my father called in to see his uncle [and aunt] and met Krause for the first time.

The Indictment claims that on that occasion, Dr. Flörsheim told my father about Krause's high rank in the former SDP, that he was actively pursuing his efforts to re-establish the party and that he, Flörsheim, was supporting him in his activities. A year later in October 1935, while both my parents were visiting the Flörsheims as an engaged couple, Dr. Flörsheim asked my father to join him on a trip to meet Krause in Tetschen. He also asked him to confirm the visit by writing a telegram as Krause had requested, and sign it under an alias, which my father did. Looking for a pretext for the visit, Dr. Flörsheim suggested my father bring along his sign-painting device so they could say they were trying to sell it abroad if stopped by the Gestapo.

The legal document states that upon arrival in Tetschen, Krause, Strauss and Flörsheim went to a café where they discussed the political situation in Germany. Krause expressed the view that economic hardships and food shortages were creating the right conditions to incite the German population into taking strike action.

F&F had highlighted the following section concerning my father with a bright yellow marker.

"Strauss, on his own initiative, described how he imagined it would first be necessary to quickly eliminate Adolph Hitler and other leaders. Krause disagreed with Strauss, saying that this would only happen at the end."

"The accused is essentially confessing."

In making the trip with his uncle and contributing to treasonous conversations, my father was deemed guilty of conspiring to commit high treason against The Third Reich by his participation in a meeting with enemies of the state.

Clearly, the Indictment differed from my father's statement to the Halle magistrate; my father wrote to exonerate his "involuntary" trip to Tetschen; he wanted to explain to the court how his uncle played on his feelings of indebtedness to manipulate him into joining him on the trip and how his aunt's pleas had led to his ultimate capitulation. The Indictment, on the other hand, looking for a conviction, rode roughshod over my father's agonized indecision which preceded his agreement. Yet, what I learnt from the Indictment that my father had not mentioned in his letter, was Krause's request to have the meeting in Tetschen confirmed by telegram, and Dr. Flörsheim's instruction to my father to write and sign it under a false name. Thus, I wondered why my father hadn't tried to justify such an incriminating act and, also, why he hadn't mentioned my mother's presence at the Flörsheims.

In subsequent phone calls and emails Noemi and I discussed the absurd allegations for which my father had paid such a high price, yet we also questioned how he could have allowed himself to go with his uncle Gustav to meet an outlawed political opponent of the Nazis, when he surely knew the regime would not tolerate any opposition. And who was this relative whom we felt was responsible for coercing his nephew into such a dangerous mission?

Noemi, who stayed in contact with my parents' overseas relatives, got in touch with my father's cousin Hattie in the US who confirmed that Gustav was my father's uncle by marriage (and also hers). He was the husband of their aunt Hilde whom my father had mentioned in his letter to the Halle magistrate, though not by name. Hattie said the Flörsheims, together with their only child, a girl, had not been able to escape from Germany and perished in concentration camp.

About a month after the arrival of the Bill of Indictment, Facts and Files got in touch again, this time to inform me that the additional material on my parents in the Federal Archives was now collated. They suggested that some of the data was sensitive and would be better explained in person.

Noemi and I resolved to travel to Berlin and see first hand the "sensitive" material Facts and Files referred to.

We began planning our trip so that my flight from Israel and hers from Australia would arrive in Frankfurt at roughly the same time. From there we would travel to Berlin together.

We were excited; it had been years since we'd spent time together without children and husbands. Yet, alongside our excitement we acknowledged the irony of the situation. In 1939 our parents and their families had been loathed and unwanted citizens in their own country. Almost sixty-five years later we, their children, were being invited back.

Noemi had visited Germany twice before and three decades earlier I had been sent by the BBC to Mainz for a day to collect some films. However, that hurried assignment didn't seem to count. I saw mostly the cabin of the plane and the interior of the Mainz offices. For all intents and purposes the forthcoming trip to my parents' homeland would be my first.

I spotted Noemi at Frankfurt airport and made a bee-line for her. We fell on each other's shoulders as we always do after an extended period of separation. Oddly, the warm, reassuring embrace brought to mind the fraught emotional reunions that had punctuated our parents' three-year ordeal when they were not allowed physical contact. I don't remember what we talked about on the flight to Berlin though we chatted non-stop.

Our meeting with Facts and Files was scheduled for two days after we arrived, leaving time on our first day for my sister to show me something of the city. With our good comprehension of the language and her spoken German we had no trouble getting around and often, I felt, passed as locals.

On a sunny, though still cool morning in late Spring, 2003 as we strolled through central Berlin's bustling shopping center looking at the attractive display windows, I tried picturing myself walking these streets as a Jew in the 1930s. There was nothing immediately obvious to conjure up those dark times which made it difficult to comprehend the hatred and anti-Semitic past of this city in which seventy percent of German Jews had once lived.

After we treated ourselves to some excellent German pastries and coffee, we headed for the beautiful synagogue in Oranienburgerstrasse, which had been bombed in 1943 but had since been restored to its original magnificence. It was one of the few Jewish houses of prayer that had not been set alight on Kristallnacht, thanks, apparently, to the bravery of the chief of the local police precinct who took on the rabble and won.

From the synagogue we made our way to the Jewish Museum, a more recent monument with a modern exterior of concrete and reflective steel, that architect Daniel Libeskind designed to represent the concept of a void. And, indeed, Noemi and I felt the emptiness he intended. At the same time, the purposefully uneven floors of the museum, both inside and out, create a sense of uneasiness and physical insecurity, a feeling of being off-balance, redolent of Nazi times.

The following morning we set out for the Facts and Files offices traveling first on the underground (U-Bahn) which connected with a bus that took us to within a few blocks of our hosts' premises in Pankow, formerly a part of East Berlin. With the help of a map and a few directions from friendly passers-by we soon found the street we were looking for, Pestalozzistrasse, a quiet, tree-lined, suburban thoroughfare with tastefully refurbished, double-story houses on each side. We assumed the renovations had been done since Germany's reunification or else had once belonged to communist apparatchiks, since in other parts of Pankow stood rows of high rise, shabby and neglected apartment blocks typical of the communist era.

We were met at the Facts and Files offices by the smiling faces of two young men who identified themselves as Frank Drauschke and Matthias Barelkowski, with whom I had corresponded. They ushered us through several high-ceilinged, smartly renovated offices they said had once been the living rooms of a large old house. In one, four chairs had been arranged around a low round table displaying a delicious looking cake. They asked us to sit down while Frank went to get a pot of coffee.

Though I tried to look calm, I wasn't. And though Noemi looked reasonably relaxed I knew she was as eager as I was for the meeting to begin. The night before we'd talked about what we might learn and we had wondered what our father would say if he were alive and what our mother would think if she could understand the purpose of our visit. Now, sitting in the F&F research bureau I had to admit it didn't bother me.

As told in "A Late Journey," the visit to Berlin would prove to be a complete eye-opener that would eventually fill in countless details of our parents' experiences.

Matthias, who nursed a large black folder on his lap, began by explaining that it contained a collection of photocopies of Gestapo documents pertaining to my mother, father, his aunt and uncle and various other people implicated in my father's case. Continuing in his slightly halting English, Matthias told us the material augmented the Bill of Indictment; amongst other things there were my mother's and my father's interrogations, their statements, an extended version of my father's letter to the Halle magistrate, selected interrogations of Gustav Flörsheim, court reports on those charged, including his wife Hilde, and the court's summing up and sentencing at my father's trial–the main hearing. He advised there wouldn't be time to go into detail about everything but the dossier was ours to take away.

These formerly classified files, he said, which had been confiscated by the Russians and taken to East Germany after the war, had lain in East German vaults from the end of 1945 to the fall of the Berlin wall in 1989. Thereafter, they had become the property of a united Germany. Matthias reminded me that F&F had been able to access the documents through my written permission as a bona fide family member.

Frank warned us we would encounter "evidence" which was probably contrived to make my father's case look worse because he was a Jew. As he said the word "Jew," I was struck by how easily the word rolled off his tongue and by how comfortable he appeared discussing the past evils of his country which even his parents may have been too young to experience personally.

He continued by suggesting we take this so-called evidence with a grain of salt, keeping in mind the malevolent regime in which the events took place. He gave the example of a statement made by a "witness" who was an inmate of Halle prison. In all likelihood, he said, this convict was an informer, placed in a cell next to my father's in order to draw him out. Apparently, the ploy bore fruit, my father supposedly confided in this total stranger and their reported conversation was added to my father's file.

Throughout our meeting, and in subsequent correspondence, Frank and Matthias referred to my parents as Irene and Gottfried; they said that during their research they felt they had come to know them and feel pity for their unfortunate entanglement with the Nazis. Perhaps intuiting our own special interest, Matthias then began to speak about my mother's attempted abortion, apologizing first for the intimate details that would be revealed. He stressed again that everything they had learned came from interrogations and investigations carried out by the Gestapo.

According to their research, my mother had become pregnant sometime in September 1935 about three months after she and my father celebrated a June engagement. Since they were considering immigrating to Palestine after their wedding planned for the end of the year, and felt a baby would be an encumbrance to work and survival in a new country, they decided to have the pregnancy terminated.

Because abortion was illegal, my father wrote to his aunt asking her to inquire if her husband, a general physician, would be prepared to perform an abortion. Dr. Gustav Flörsheim refused. As a result, my father hired a charlatan who'd apparently performed a successful abortion on the girlfriend of one of his acquaintances. Without administering an anesthetic and using bare hands, this "doctor," who charged them forty Reichmarks for his "work," introduced a rubber tube into my mother and proceeded to pump into her hot soapy water which was supposed to dislodge the fetus. The "operation" failed, and some days later the excruciating procedure was repeated. It, too, did not produce the desired results but left my mother with a serious ovarian infection.

Noemi and I were spellbound, hardly able to look at one another. I'd have stopped Matthias right there in order to stay with this sad and shocking news for a few moments longer but I realized there would be time for that afterwards, and in any event, Matthias indicated he had more to convey. As he did, I had to make a special effort to steer my thoughts away from the procedure he had just described.

The young couple then turned for help to my father's uncle. They drove to Zeitz which I remembered my mother had mentioned in one of her letters, so that he could examine her and treat her for the infection. They initially tried to conceal the fact that an abortion had already been attempted and it seems my father asked Gustav to reconsider performing one. But he again refused though he treated my mother's illness. Since she was too sick to travel, my father's aunt, Hilde, offered to keep her and my father at their place until her condition improved. It was during the time my mother was convalescing at the Flörsheim's that Gustav asked my father to accompany him on the car trip to meet Franz Krause in Tetschen.

It occurred to me that the attempted abortion might explain the six months sentence my father served before his main trial. I asked Matthias about this, but he said it wasn't the case. My parents, he said, were acquitted of the charge of incitement to abortion without any explanation given by the court as to how or why it had arrived at its verdict. Instead, however, my father had committed an infringement of the Nazi laws governing foreign exchange and was found guilty of profiteering from foreign currency. He served six months for this misdemeanor. Matthias told us he'd found a 1936 entry in the public prosecutor's office in Duisburg to this effect but that this charge also, came without any clarification.

By far the most serious charge Frank pointed out, and that made up the bulk of the dossier, was the one which brought with it a conviction of high treason, handed down at my father's main hearing on 29th January 1937, by the Supreme Court of Prussia (to which the district of Halle belonged). There wasn't much I could ask about the legal aspects of high treason in The Third Reich because there hadn't been time in between the arrival of the Bill of Indictment and our visit to Berlin to bone up on Nazi criminal law. Nevertheless, our hosts explained that because Nazi Germany was a totalitarian state, accusations of disloyalty and betrayal were common during the period and brought with them especially stiff prison sentences.

I returned to my father's conviction and wondered aloud whether he had tried to smuggle money out of the country in the event of having to flee or whether, alternatively, he had tried to exchange money on the black market. Unfortunately, neither Frank nor Matthias could throw any light on the matter.

Near the end of our meeting I suddenly realized I hadn't flipped the tape I'd set up to record our conversation, which was regrettable, because I'd also stopped taking comprehensive notes. Clearly, my years of experience as a radio and television interviewer had not helped when the subject matter touched me so personally. Thankfully, I had Noemi's excellent memory to rely on to reconstruct our exchange.

Before the meeting drew to a close Frank invited us to join them for lunch the next day, followed by a visit to the Federal Archives. They offered to show us some of the originals of the documents included in the dossier.

I could hardly wait to be alone with Noemi, to collect my thoughts and combine them with the information we had from the letters. As I recalled my initial reaction to my mother's first mention of the attempted abortion, I realized my earlier theories were false. No Nazi had forced an abortion on my mother and no medical experiments had been performed either, other than the one attempted by the quack. I was dismayed by my own naiveté, by the fact that I had not been able to countenance the possibility that my young mother would agree to an abortion. I still found it hard to believe she would allow some amateur near her.

Noemi raised the matter of a dead baby boy my mother mentioned during a family summer holiday by the beach, and wondered whether it was the same child. I suggested that losing the baby in about the fifth month of pregnancy might also explain why the authorities did not press charges since no actual abortion was concluded. Or had a sympathetic Nazi judge, if there ever was such a creature, taken pity on my parents who had already suffered the loss of their baby?

It now seemed as though my mother's mystery illness might have been the lingering effects of an ovarian infection. This assumption related to the only clue I'd picked up from one of my mother's letters in which she'd written my father that *one side has responded positively to treatment while the other is still inflamed.* At the time, I thought she might be referring to her lungs, since she often experienced a persistent, irritating cough.

My sister and I talked our way through dinner and sat on our hotel beds chatting late into the night. We kept returning to the attempted abortion and the ensuing infection which we now understood had led my father into the arms of his uncle Gustav at the very time he was planning his dangerous trip to Tetschen. In fact, I wondered whether my father had initially refused to accompany his uncle, as he'd stated in his letter to the Halle magistrate, because he didn't want to leave his sick fiancée, with his reservations about the trip's risky undertaking a secondary consideration. And we now understood that he hadn't mentioned my mother's presence in his letter to the Halle magistrate, probably for fear of drawing attention to the reason they had visited his aunt and uncle in the first place.

Before we turned in for the night we flipped through some of the sections of the dossier easily identifying those which F&F had marked in English; Police Interrogation of Gottfried Strauss, Police Interrogation of Irene Strauss, Warrant of Arrest and so on. We didn't much bother trying to read the German because we were thoroughly exhausted and in any case, I was going to translate it. The next morning we set out to meet our hosts for an early lunch at a pub which served authentic German frankfurters and sauerkraut. After a leisurely meal, we headed for our destination within easy walking distance.

The German Federal Archives are located in Lichterfelde, an outer suburb of Berlin about half an hour by train from the center of the city. I expected to find an imposing, late nineteenth century edifice built in the neo-classical style of the Reichstag. To my great surprise, the Archives are a dispersed collection of plain, domestic-style, two-storey, red brick buildings situated in the rolling grounds of a high-walled compound once used as an army barracks. The ordinariness of their exterior, however, belies the secret treasures the library is preserving for posterity in a massive paper collection of such enormous physical weight that only the ground floor is able to support it. The administrative offices are situated on the upper level.

We were shown into the entrance by Frank and Matthias, veterans of this venerable institution, and then led to the chief librarian who gave us each a pair of white cotton gloves to put on in order to protect the documents. She then left us to our experienced researchers.

Frank took us into a reading room while Matthias went to requisition the relevant files. A few minutes later, with awkwardly gloved hands, we were skimming through the original pages they had promised to show us. Frank found us the seventeen page document my father had handwritten which, he explained, was an expanded version of his plea to the Halle magistrate, this time he was addressing the Examining Magistrate of the Peoples' Court, a kangaroo court Hitler created to control the entire Nazi judiciary.

Noemi and I sat quietly in the rarified atmosphere of the room. I resisted the urge to remove my glove and run my fingers lightly over my father's words, as though by touching his writing I could get closer to him.

Only the odd word was instantly recognizable while the rest of the writing swam before my eyes, but it didn't matter. I had seen the original plea and, in any case, I would spend long hours translating the material. I noticed that apart from my father's handwritten letter the rest of the files were typed, all of them being official documents. But, I can't honestly say I took much in.

It was an awe-inspiring experience simply sitting in the presence of evidence that had been recorded and used to torment my defenseless parents.

Occasionally, one of us asked Frank or Matthias for an explanation of a stamp or a signature but other than that we did not speak and they did not disturb us.

I again thought of my mother. What would she say or think if she were able to comprehend the significance of this afternoon? And would my father, in his wildest imagination, ever have dreamt during the writing of his hopeless plea for justice, that his daughters would one day see it with their own eyes?

The visit to the Archives, which took less than an hour, enabled us to pay our last respects to the bureaucratic remains of an episode in our parents' history they had so assiduously kept from us, but whose ramifications, nonetheless, we had experienced indirectly in their personalities and in their behavior towards us and each other.

Before saying our goodbyes to Frank and Matthias we enquired about the possibility of further research on my grandfather, Karl Strauss. They had come across some tax files of his which we'd noticed the night before included at the back of the dossier. Frank said he believed there was more material available and as soon as they had accessed it they would let me know.

Noemi and I were pleased we'd left time in our original plan for more sightseeing which also gave us the opportunity before leaving Germany to get used to some of the things we'd learned.

In the remaining days, we took a leisurely walk down the famous boulevard, Unter Den Linden, the pedestrian mall flanked by buildings of grandeur and elegance such as the State Opera and State Library as well as by modern shops, cafes, restaurants and hotels. Before Kristallnacht, which obliterated any traces of its former Jewish character, Unter Den Linden had been a centre of Jewish life and business.

We also visited the planned site of the Topography of Terror exhibition which commemorates the location where Hitler's SS masterminded the twelve-year reign of terror that led to the extermination of six million Jews and countless other victims.

Our last stop took us to the remains of the Berlin Wall and Checkpoint Charlie, the former security barrier and gate that had divided the nation into East and West Germany for over thirty years during the Cold War. These days, a section of the wall and the security checkpoint are a popular tourist attraction.

At the end of five days Noemi and I returned to Israel where she spent a week with me and my husband before flying back to Australia. Strangely, during that time we hardly looked at the Federal Archives dossier other than to show it to my husband. I needed some distance from it in order to prepare for the job ahead; Noemi was quite happy to wait until she could read the documents in English.

In due course, I took on the arduous, though exhilarating task of translating the hefty–in both weight and substance–dossier, welcoming the chance once again, to further polish my German. Yet the work, obviously, held more significance than a mere exercise in translation and as I flipped back and forth between the dossier and my parents' letters, cross-referencing events, checking a point here and there, I shuddered. Trying to put myself in my parents' shoes during the several interrogations to which the Gestapo had subjected them was painful beyond words.

And indeed, when I eventually traveled to Halle some time much later I was shown written evidence, not included in the F&F material, that my father had on one occasion, at least, been brought to a section of the prison where it had been standard practice to torture prisoners during interrogation. The thought of it made me ill.

Alongside a sense of awe that my young parents had withstood questioning by the Nazis, and that my father had survived torture, I felt some satisfaction that, despite their unwillingness to talk about the past, I now had a source of information about their years in Nazi Germany thanks not only to the Germans' meticulous record keeping, but also to the researchers who had unearthed it.

Thus, in this voluminous document from the Berlin archives I became privy to the drama that was being played out behind the scenes of their letters.

My parents' interrogations are written up as monologues. At no time are the interrogator's questions included although occasionally they are implied in the testimony by the use of the conditional phrase, "If it is put to me that…then my response is…" It is uncertain whether the transcriptions are my parents' actual words, or edited summaries composed by someone else adopting the grammatical form of the first person singular.

My father's depositions are signed by two people and my mother's by one, though this doesn't necessarily indicate how many people were present during their questioning. There is no reference to the setting or to the time taken by the interrogation. However, occasionally there is a break "due to the late hour." Sometimes I think I recognize some of my parents' German expressions.

My relatively broad reading on the Nazi era indicated that these records were compiled and preserved by the minions of a fascist dictatorship who dispensed a version of law corrupted by political terror and rabid anti-Semitism.

According to Nikolaus Wachsmann's " Hitler's Prisons, Legal Terror in Nazi Germany," published by Yale University Press, 2004, citizens like my parents and the Flörsheims were singled out by the Nazis for "special treatment as community aliens," a term applied by the authorities to a multitude of individuals including 'racial aliens' [like Jews or Poles], political prisoners and various criminal offenders: there was a considerable overlap in Nazi thinking about these different groups, with criminal, racial and political categories often merging into one: Jews were not only seen as a racial danger, they were also described as the political enemies of Nazism, behind Communism and Liberalism, and as a criminal menace blamed for much common crime."

In the first years of Nazism, Jews arrested by the police and sentenced by the courts were more likely to be persecuted for their political opposition to the regime, rather than as racial aliens, which was, apparently, the case with Gustav and Hilde Flörsheim and my parents.

High treason, the crime for which they were convicted was regarded not just as an attack on the rulers but on the entire "national community." As Frank and Matthias had mentioned, it demanded especially harsh sentences which the anti-Semitic and anti-Communist judges handed down with impunity.

What continued to astonish was the amount of time and energy the system invested in grilling ordinary, private individuals like my parents, and attributing to them political motives which neither of them had. My mother was never remotely interested in politics and my father's interest arose chiefly from the way in which politics influenced the economy. Even Gustav Flörsheim's reasons for being involved with Franz Krause turned out to be more complex than I at first discerned.

In trying to win a conviction for high treason, the Gestapo concentrated their questioning of each suspect on four main issues surrounding the trip to Tetschen; the purpose of the trip, the political conversations held there, the telegram written to confirm the trip and my father's sign-painting device as a cover for the journey.

Though the dossier contained material about several other people unknown to me who were involved in some way with Gustav Flörsheim and Franz Krause, I have chosen to concentrate on the interrogations and statements of my parents and Gustav, and to a lesser extent on his wife, Hilde, because they were family closely involved in my father's tragedy. My father's interrogation took place thirteen days after he was arrested.

Interrogation of Gottfried Strauss, 20th December 1935

"I didn't want to go (to Tetschen) but my uncle persuaded me that the contact with Krause would prove useful in furthering my patenting business and, in addition, he wanted me to shoulder the petrol costs. Also, my aunt begged me to go along to placate her husband."

"At the instigation of my uncle I wrote a telegram to Krause announcing that we would be arriving the following Sunday. I told my uncle that if I signed the telegram in my own name Krause would not know who it was from to which he replied that I should sign it 'Marianne' and Krause would recognize its sender."

"When we arrived in Tetschen we met Krause in the market place and the three of us went to a café where, during a discussion about the war in Abyssinia, Krause expressed the view that the fascist regimes of Italy and Germany could be overthrown.

My uncle and Krause then discussed Germany's present day difficulties, the food shortage, the scarcity of raw materials and the price rises. Krause said that this unrest would lead to a strike which would encourage the population to stage protests and the rest would follow. My constant objections annoyed my uncle who said I didn't understand much about these things."

"Krause and my uncle also talked of espionage, Krause claiming that, as head of illegal work, he appointed people to various secret jobs assisted by his contacts at the highest level of the SA (Storm Troopers) and the Military."

"We spoke of my uncle's interest in Krause finding him a similar position to his own to which I commented that my uncle's (sexual) indiscretions alone would never make him a suitable candidate for this type of work."

Later, in my father's long statement to the Peoples' Court he wrote about his uncle that, had he been free to indulge his sexual passions with Aryan women, contrary to the dictates of the Nüremberg Laws, he would have gladly laid aside his political aspirations and his friendship with Franz Krause who had apparently promised to help him win a political position. My father continues:

"The two men then went off together, my uncle explaining, 'we must leave you alone now, later you can present your sign-painting device.' I felt like the fifth wheel and it became clear to me that Krause and Gustav went off without me so that Gustav could convey to Krause treasonable information from Germany."

"Henceforth, I had no more interest in presenting my sign-painting device to Krause since it seemed absurd to me to enter into any business dealings with a partner like him."

"Prior to our departure, Krause told my uncle that he ought to wait and see how things developed in his medical practice before considering a political appointment."

Interestingly, my father was not asked to account for his apparent suggestion stated in the Bill of Indictment that Hitler should be assassinated. And I wondered whether he'd have used a word as damning as "treasonable" when describing Gustav's private conversations with Krause since, he too, had participated in these conversations. But this was before I realized my father had little cause to spare his uncle.

If the transcriptions of the interrogations can be believed, which is not at all certain, other remarks my father apparently made about espionage are contradictory.

The court made much of my father's sign-painting device being the pretext for the journey to Tetschen, in spite of his protests that his uncle had persuaded him to take it along so that Krause could advise him on how to market it abroad, an idea which undoubtedly appealed to my father's business instincts. It seemed feasible, that, when he recognized that Krause was more of a political activist than a businessman, he decided not to seek his advice. Yet, the court dismissed my father's explanation since Gustav had insisted during his interrogation that the device was, indeed, the cover for the journey and it suited the court to go along with that.

My father then speaks about the attempted abortion:

"Before my fiancée missed her period in mid-September 1935, we had intended to emigrate. I had her examined by a Dr. Regensteiner who could not confirm she was pregnant. I then wrote to my aunt Hilde asking whether uncle Gustav was prepared to do an abortion and she replied that he wasn't, though he offered to drive us to Karlsbad, Czechoslovakia, to see a Dr. Stern, which I rejected. My fiancée and I then drove to my uncle's place in Zeitz so that he could examine her to establish whether or not she was, in fact, pregnant. In case it turned out that she was, and we changed our minds about going to Karlsbad, I obtained a letter of credit to be supplied in Czech kroners."

"In response to my uncle's statement (that must have been read out to my father) that he knew an intervention had taken place on the growing fetus which had resulted in a suppurating inflammation of my wife's ovaries, I say the following: I did initially lie to him but only in order to mislead him. I wanted him to treat her because she was very unwell. I considered the infection to be the result of a chill. In any event no illegal abortion took place on my wife."

Three days later on 23rd December 1935, my father was again called to an interrogation, only this time he had requested it.

"I registered an hour ago for interrogation because I want to make a confession. In consideration of my wife I have, up until now, not told the truth since I wanted to spare her any further grief."

"When I first wrote to my uncle requesting an abortion on my wife and he refused, I approached a friend who referred me to an abortionist (my father supplied names and addresses of both men), who subsequently carried out the two procedures in my apartment."

In all their painful details, almost word for word as it had been told to us by Facts and Files in Berlin, my father then described the interventions.

Driven by fear and desperation after some of Gustav's interrogation had been read out to him, my father attempted to persuade his uncle to tell the truth about his essential innocence, politically speaking, by trying to smuggle a letter to him in another part of the prison. It was his one opportunity to express his anger. The undated letter (written after 20th December 1935, and before 20th March 1936, when he was still unaware of my mother's miscarriage) was intercepted and added to my father's file:

D. Gustav,

I am taking the risk of writing to you. I hope you never use this (against me) and will be careful in your answer never to get caught…This is a frightful catastrophe in which we are all to be pitied. Yet the difference between us is that you dragged me into this thing. Six days after my wedding, arrested; in May we are expecting a child which I may not see, my youthful fortune! Everything is ruined because of you. In any case, I don't want to reproach you, rather I have a request: answer my questions honestly. Because you have seriously burdened me you owe it to me to be honest. Of course, I know you have burdened me. Even the officer asked me whether you have a particular interest in burdening me. So I beg you not to make me out a liar and to find the courage to vouch for me. Actually I couldn't tell them anything new; they knew everything down to the smallest detail.

Twice questioned on 20th December 1935, I admitted that your basic convictions made you an enemy of the state but you didn't busy yourself with me. I merely said that you communicated with Krause from time to time and that you told me a lot of things, but they were things in which you were not involved. I can't say anything else because I don't know anything else as far as political matters are concerned. In my opinion, the matter is only very serious if one has done something. They knew that you had brought money from Tetschen to Halle but apart from that they did not ask me whether you had done this or that. But I did admit that you were offered a position. I ask you once again urgently to answer the questions in this letter with the utmost honesty and sincerity:

Did you say my sign-painting device was taken on the journey as a cover for making the trip?

Were you asked whether I knew what Krause did abroad before I went on the trip?

Were you asked whether I agreed with your views? I remind you of my words of warning in the car.

Do you think Krause is in prison?

Did you ever tell me what sort of a position you were being offered?

Were you asked whether I arranged for an abortion and if so, what did you say?

The inspector read out word for word your following statement: "There was also talk in Tetschen about military matters like underground aeroplane hangars, Leuna etc. My nephew was present on this occasion." Is this correct? I can really swear that I heard nothing about this. I beg you again urgently to vouch for me.

During my entire interrogation I could only report what Krause told us. In all good conscience I was not able to say that you or I gave Krause any piece of news. That butter is scarce and that there are dissatisfied people, the inspector said was inconsequential. Were you asked about that and what did you say?

Unfortunately, my father grossly overestimated both his uncle's humanity and the benevolence of the Nazis. He also failed to realize that when he informed the Gestapo that Gustav's "basic convictions made [him] an enemy of the state," simply by virtue of being a Jew, he too, belonged in the same category.

That he believed "the matter is only very serious if one has done something" shows a failure to grasp the viciousness of a system bent on weeding out and persecuting all those whom it considered to be non-Aryans.

Although Gustav's interrogations appear in the dossier, the details of his trial and sentencing do not. The timing of his interrogations at first confused me because they were dated after my father's, which didn't explain how the investigating officer had been able to read a section of them out to my father. I then realized that Facts and Files had included Gustav's re-interrogations, carried out more than a year after the first ones.

Interrogations of Gustav Flörsheim 21st and 23rd December 1936 and 4th January 1937.

"At the beginning of September (1935), Strauss wrote me that his fiancée was pregnant. When they both came to my place I did not perform an abortion. I treated Irene Meyer for an inflammation which was the result of an attempted abortion."

"My refusal to perform an abortion on Irene Meyer was based on my opinion that Strauss was in a position to marry her. When I examined her and found that she had a right-sided ovarian inflammation and was in fact two months pregnant I asked her whether an abortion had been attempted and she replied that it had not. However, some time later she admitted to the attempt, adding that she and her husband did not yet want a child."

"Strauss asked me yet again to perform an abortion but I refused because this would have been impossible given Irene Meyer's state of health. I want to note here that no abortion took place in the time that followed and Irene Meyer had the child."

Gustav had been in prison since 22nd November 1935, and therefore did not know that my mother had suffered a miscarriage. The date also indicated that at the time of my parents' wedding on 1st December 1935, they knew that Gustav had been arrested. This knowledge must have dampened their joy and not just because Gustav was a relative. I cannot believe that my father was not worried that, by association, he too would be called in for interrogation. My mother, though, in all innocence, says in her interrogation that the possibility of my father being arrested did not cross her mind.

"The journey to Tetschen to see Franz Krause was undertaken for illegal purposes. In a postcard that arrived at my place while Strauss and his fiancée were staying with us, Krause informed me he was awaiting my arrival in Tetschen and asked for confirmation of this arrangement by telegram."

"I naturally assumed he had a (political) position for me and so I sent him a telegram signed 'Marianne' saying I would be there on 3rd November 1935, between 14:00 and 15:00 hours. I dictated the contents to Strauss who wrote it in his own hand because I wanted to avoid a situation in which, through my handwriting, my connection to Krause would be known."

"Despite having knowledge of Krause's activities and my collaboration with him, Strauss had no misgivings about coming along. His statement that he joined me on the journey because he wanted Krause's opinion about his sign-painting device is untrue. This was merely a camouflage. He came with me so that in the event of our reason for the trip being discovered he could refute it. The disguise was my suggestion and Strauss agreed. At first, Strauss did not show Krause the device because as I have said it was a cover but I myself, shortly before our departure, showed it to him in Strauss's presence since I wanted to know once and for all whether it had any commercial value."

"When we got to Tetschen we met Krause and the three of us went to a café. Krause spoke of his illegal travels but did not mention which people he came in contact with. After we had coffee I went to move my car leaving Strauss and Krause alone for about half an hour."

"In the evening during a two hour dinner Krause and Strauss conducted a long conversation in which Strauss asked Krause about the unrest in Germany and the possibility of pogroms taking place. Krause said he didn't believe that would happen and asked Strauss about his own business activities. Strauss told him he'd been a department manager in a retail store to which Krause replied he could possibly arrange similar employment in Russia. The place was full and there was a lot of noise. I busied myself with thoughts about my own future because Krause had told me earlier in the day that he had no political job for me."

"I cannot say why Strauss received an offer from Krause. These two must have discussed this right down to the last detail when I went to shift my car after we'd had coffee earlier in the day."

"The next day we arranged to meet again for lunch in the hotel. Before lunch I showed Krause two models of Strauss's sign-painting device in my room in Strauss's absence. I think Krause told Strauss that at a later opportunity he could do something with it."

Gustav Flörsheim's words about my father present him as an informed and willing accomplice to a dangerous political mission. I am not aware that my father ever did anything to harm his uncle yet the doctor seemed to show no compunction about betraying his young nephew and seeing him go down with him. Later, the story about the sign-painting device being taken along as a cover provided the Gestapo with ammunition to set the accused against one another. Also, I wondered whether Gustav had used incriminating terminology when he referred to the trip to Tetschen as one undertaken for 'illegal' purposes or whether the Gestapo was taking gross liberties with the evidence presented.

The uncle's claim that my father "had no misgivings" about going to Tetschen flatly contradicts my father's statement to the Halle magistrate, and later, my mother's account of the evening in question. And whether he'd actually shown Krause my father's sign-painting device is a moot point. My father claimed he did not show Krause the device at all.

Yet, perhaps Gustav's most outrageous insinuation is that my father was interested in a job in Russia; my father was no less suspicious of communism than he was of fascism. Of course, Krause may very well have made an offer but that did not prove that my father was remotely interested in living in Russia. However, Gustav was clever enough to imply that he was, and not only interested, but keen enough "to have discussed this [with him] right down to the last detail."

Interrogation of Irene Strauss 29th February and 2nd March 1936.

My mother's interrogation took place in Oberhausen prison where she was being held in a cell after the miscarriage she suffered in hospital. It was early on in my father's detention during the time he did not hear from her for several weeks.

The files indicated that two days before the Gestapo questioned her they searched "the apartment of the couple Strauss." This must have been my father's apartment where my parents intended to live after their wedding, and where my mother had evidently already shifted her belongings. What they found there and made a great fuss about is beyond absurd. A report on their findings was attached to my mother's interrogation with a cover letter stamped and underlined <u>Secret! (Geheim)</u>.

The letter was addressed to the Examining Judge of the Peoples' Court, Director Bork of the District Court in Berlin, regarding the criminal case against Irene Strauss from Oberhausen and others, for the preparation of treason and high treason. I was shocked to see my mother, also, had been charged with this crime.

The results of the search included:

"Two picture postcards of German armored cruisers…they were post-marked Hamburg June 1934. The photos may already have been used for purposes of high treason or its intention."

My mother's response to the search:

"These photos of the armored cruiser 'Deutschland' naming the armaments it is equipped with were sent last year by my brother Eric Meyer in Hamburg to my father who is very interested in war history. Because I liked these photos I pasted them in my album. They were not intended to be forwarded to Uncle Gustav, or through my husband, to Franz Krause."

Leaving no stone unturned, the Secret Police paid a visit to my mother's brother in Hamburg on 19th March 1936, in order to question him about the photos and search his apartment. They claimed the search did not produce any evidence that he was involved in activities hostile to the state.

Eric Meyer stated that he bought the pictures in a local photo shop and after listing the armaments, whose names he'd learned from magazines and books, sent them to his father.

To complete their farcical investigation, the Gestapo also questioned my father on 4th April 1936:

"I can only say that I never saw the pictures at my wife's place. To the claim that I spoke to my cell neighbor about them allegedly saying that I had in my possession pictures that, if discovered, would cost me my head, I must deny that. I only know that my wife's father was very interested in the details of battle so that perhaps the pictures might have been given to him. My wife definitely has no interest in them and neither do I."

The Gestapo also conducted a search in my mother's cell in Oberhausen prison: During one of the searches in her cell, a postcard was found in one of Irene Strauss's books which carries the following note in pencil: Joseph Wedlich, Praha VII,

Komenicke 1, CSR. This is the address of the communist agent Franz Krause, alias Joseph Wedlich, who is wanted by the state police in Halle. The possession of this address proves that Irene Strauss also maintained an illegal relationship with Krause, alias Wedlich.

My mother's response to the postcard stated:

"Aunt Hilde asked my husband to write to Krause, alias Wedlich, to let him know that Gustav was depressed and though my husband had written the letter he left it at my father-in-law's place and from there it was given to his defense lawyer."

No evidence was found that my mother ever met or spoke to Krause, but this didn't bother the Nazis.

Several letters were found from Karl Strauss, who lives in Kulmbach. One letter of 5th January 1936 (not in the collection) to Irene Strauss says: 'Gottfried already told me…about the strange political ideas of uncle Gustav in addition to which Gustav took him out of the country against his will.' This letter and four others that could possibly be meaningful will be confiscated.

Karl Strauss was the only person allowed to visit my father in Halle shortly after his arrest. During the visit, he apparently heard my father's version of the trip to Tetschen, which he then reported, I believe quite innocently, to my mother in his 5th January 1936 letter. Unfortunately, my father's privately expressed admission to my grandfather that his uncle took him to Tetschen "against his will" counted for nothing.

In a democratic court of law my father's comment may have been used as evidence of his innocent intentions. But the Gestapo had its own version of what constituted proof. The courtroom of The Third Reich was no arena for leniency or for assuming innocence until proven guilty. I did not see the letter referred to again in any of the protocols.

My mother continues:

"The reason we visited the Flörsheims was for me to be introduced to them and for Dr. Flörsheim to examine me to determine whether I was pregnant and to see what else might be amiss with me. He did, in fact, establish that I was pregnant and that I had an ovarian infection. My husband told him that an abortion had been attempted on me. I did not suggest a further abortion though I cannot say whether my husband did. I presume he did not."

"I wanted to go along on the trip [to Tetschen] because I didn't want my husband to travel alone. I was frightened there might be an accident and then I would be left alone with the child. I did not fear my husband would be arrested. I do not know why his uncle wanted to see the friend in Tetschen, that is, I do not know whether their meeting amounted to high treason."

My mother's poignant comment that she did not fear my father being arrested, if that is what she truly thought, suggests the same misplaced trust as her husband's, in the system which regarded them as enemies.

"I did not read the card that came from Tetschen summoning my husband's uncle to a meeting, though Uncle Gustav was very delighted at the prospect of traveling there."

"Since I was too ill to participate in the journey, I also forbade my husband (at the time, my fiancé) from going along. Uncle Gustav began to scold me, which only made me more insistent that my husband should not go, but then I had to go to bed. When my husband came to say goodnight, he assured me he would not go but in the morning he told me that his aunt had persuaded him and he had agreed out of a sense of gratitude for all the things she had done for him. I had words with his aunt but my husband went anyway, telling me he wanted to try and interest Krause in his sign-painting device."

"I can remember that the sign-painting device was taken along, in a way, as an alibi. My uncle told my husband that if the Gestapo stopped them they could say they went to Tetschen to try and interest a friend in it, though I cannot remember the exact words that Gustav used. "

Without being able to imagine what she had done, if one can believe the veracity of the protocols, which is not at all certain, my mother had, inadvertently, joined forces with Gustav against my father. Though she hadn't exactly said it was my father's "intention" to use the device as an alibi, she apparently heard the idea expressed by Gustav. The sign-painting device could easily have been taken to Tetschen to serve both goals; to interest Franz Krause in marketing it and to use it as a cover for the journey.

"When my husband and his uncle returned from Tetschen my husband told me that Krause thought the sign-painting device quite good and that he believed it should be further developed in Germany."

Yet, my father had stated that he didn't show Krause the device after he realized Krause was an enemy agent. He did not say that someone else (Gustav) had.

"If I am asked what the sign-painting device was supposed to cover up and what the reason for going to Tetschen was, I can only say that Gustav was supposed to get an offer to work on Krause's uncle's newspaper."

When my father was questioned again about the sign-painting device he answered:

"In response to my wife's statement that my sign-painting device was taken to Tetschen as a pretext, I can only say that this definitely does not express the truth. Uncle Gustav mentioned that idea for the first time in the car on our return journey."

The Gestapo had succeeded in pitting my parents against one another over this ridiculous matter and the court then used their conflicting statements to "prove" my father was a traitor.

<u>A Warrant of Arrest</u> dated 4th March 1936 and marked "Secret" was issued for my father (and eight others) about three months after he was apprehended. Though Gustav and Hilde appear on the same warrant, Gustav's case was heard in a separate trial in Berlin. Despite the charges and her interrogation as a suspect, the Warrant named my mother only as a witness.

All nine accused were connected in some way to people who had contact with supporters of the outlawed Social Democratic Party in which Franz Krause was a leading light. They were suspected of being accomplices in the preparation for treason and high treason against The Third Reich, according to section 47 of the criminal code, paragraphs 80-88. Descriptions of the character and behavior of the nine were written up in a document dated 28th February 1936, and sent to the offices of the Gestapo in the district of Merseburg, for forwarding to the State Attorney of the Reich.

Five out of the nine accused were Jews. This was not surprising because Gustav Flörsheim involved members of his extended family in his dealings with Franz Krause.

Though my father and his aunt and uncle, amongst others, were initially apprehended and sentenced for suspected political opposition to the Nazis, there was not even an attempt to disguise the vicious anti-Semitism inherent in the legal system.

"The many sided criminal activities of the Jews proves that they were determined under all circumstances to harm the German Reich in every imaginable way. In most cases, their interrogations were taken with extreme difficulty, as comes to light in the files, in that everything they were accused of they flatly denied. There could hardly be any better evidence that emphasizes the inferiority of the Jewish race than the matter at hand."

The Warrant's comments on Gustav, Hilde and my father:

Flörsheim, Gustav.

"Flörsheim did not belong to a political party before the radical change (Hitler's takeover), although he wore the badge of the SPD and placed his ads in the communist newspaper AIZ (Arbeiter Illustrierte Zeitung). His Marxist outlook is generally known. Since the summer of 1933, he has been in contact with Franz Krause who himself joined the KPD (Communist party). During their illegal activities in Germany Flörsheim sent Krause, who without a doubt was already in the service of the Czech and Russian governments at the time, news, which, in the interests of national defense, was supposed to be kept a secret. He also pulled his relatives into activities hostile to the state.

Furthermore, for the purposes of pursuing his subversive political activities he committed race defilement with Franz Krause's girlfriend, Hanni S and his former receptionist Nora K."

According to my father's statement to the People's Court, Gustav committed race defilement because of his pronounced sexual appetite for non-Jewish women and not because the affairs led him to politics. It can be assumed that he wanted Krause to find him political work outside Germany so that he could pursue his affairs unencumbered by the Nüremberg Laws which, inside Germany, hampered his sexual freedom. It appears the Laws were one of the key reasons for his disenchantment with the National Socialists. That the Nazis also made his medical profession impossible may have been an additional factor though my father didn't say this. His alleged Marxist leanings and support of Germany's former Communist party would not have endeared him to the National Socialists. The report continues:

"He brought treasonable written material and illegal monies into Germany from Czechoslovakia and donated his own money to the Red Aid (Rote Hilfe)."

"Flörsheim admitted that on two occasions he had taken between 500-600RM out of the German Reich without permission and sent it to America via Czechoslovakia."

"In his capacity as a doctor he repeatedly committed a wrong of the most serious kind. He was convicted of performing three abortions."

"Flörsheim, a man who is extremely sly and deceitful, at first denied all the accusations brought against him. Only after he was presented with circumstantial evidence and the statements of his co-accused, as well as those of the witnesses, was he forced to make a confession."

Flörsheim, Hilde.

"Hilde Flörsheim, allegedly, was not politically active. However, in her basic convictions she shares her husband's Marxist views. She is a crafty, cunning Jewess who presents the most unimaginable difficulties in her interrogations and absolutely did not want to make any statement before first finding out what her husband had said, proving she knew of and approved of his treasonable activities."

"In the absence of her husband, she carried on negotiations in her apartment, hostile to the state, with Franz Krause. She took dictation from her husband about news that was meant for abroad and met with Franz Krause in Tetschen when she joined her husband on a trip there."

"She also had a share in his foreign currency movements."

"On her own initiative, she encouraged and promoted treasonable activities of her husband and Franz Krause."

Hilde Flörsheim's interrogations do not appear in the dossier. However, she was tried together with my father and also found guilty of high treason. The stereotypical characterization of her as a "crafty cunning Jewess," may have indicated she was an unusually strong woman who could not be intimidated. But this is guesswork. It becomes clear in my father's statement to the People's Court that he was very fond of his aunt and therefore stopped short of blaming her for his own lack of resolve. Nevertheless, she chose to put her own needs above the wishes of her nephew which led him straight into a trap.

Strauss, Gottfried.

"At the instigation of his uncle, Gustav Flörsheim, Strauss took part in activities hostile to the state. He supported these activities in that he participated in an illegal meeting with Franz Krause and also arranged for it."

"Strauss was observed, together with Flörsheim leaving Sokol House (The Central Spy Agency) in Tetschen. He disguised this visit by claiming he wanted to sell a patent for his sign-painting device."

"Strauss participated in a conversation between Flörsheim and Krause in which treasonable things were said. He had knowledge of intended sabotage, acts of violence and strikes. It is beyond doubt that Strauss was active on a far larger scale in activities hostile to the state than the outcome of the investigation up until now is able to show. It is to be assumed that the connection to the Rhineland, where the SPD is supposed to be particularly well organized, is conducted through him."

"At his instigation, an abortion was twice attempted on his bride-to-be, Irene Meyer."

"With regard to the couple Flörsheim, Gottfried Strauss and Irene Meyer (and two other indictees) the matter concerns Jews."

As can be seen, the Nazi court was prepared to convict a Jew "on the assumption" that his "crimes" were worse than they could prove. Since my father was not able to explain why he wrote the telegram to Krause other than to state that his uncle instructed him to, the Warrant conveniently accused him of arranging the Tetschen meeting, implying that he took a degree of initiative for which absolutely no evidence is presented.

There is no further comment about the alleged visit to The Central Spy Agency in Tetschen.

Attached to my father's files are the elaborate statements of a certain Heinrich L, a fellow prisoner who Frank Drauschke of Facts and Files had mentioned as a witness-cum-informer. It is worth noting what historian Nikolaus Wachsmann says about informers in The Third Reich:

"…denunciations by inmates clearly proved an important source of information for the authorities…Looking for political offences, some of the betrayers were official informers recruited by the Nazi regime. More often, prisoners denounced fellow inmates on their own initiative hoping to gain privileges or early release."

Heinrich L, a former construction worker, in prison for breaking and entering, said he shared a cell wall and a high window with my father. He claims my father made contact with him by tapping on the lower part of the wall and then continuing in an upward direction indicating his intention to speak via their common window.

Heinrich L's statement 13th February 1936:

"My cell neighbor, who I now know is called Gottfried Strauss, asked if I was here for political reasons. I said yes, even though this is not true…he then asked me whether I was anti-Semitic, which I denied…he said I'll tell you about the facts of the case;

my uncle and I moved blocks of shares to the CSR from where another man was supposed to take them to Russia."

"Strauss told me that he and his wife had bought shares from a Frau W. (a business acquaintance) who kept her considerable fortune in the United States, undeclared to the German tax authorities."

How much of this is pure invention and how much fact, can never be established.

With good reason, Frank had warned Noemi and me to take the "witness" testimonies with a grain of salt. To us, it seemed outlandish that my father would tell a perfect stranger, whom he could not even see, that he had been involved in tax fraud and ask him whether he was anti-Semitic.

In any event, Heinrich L's "evidence" fell apart when he claimed my father told him that my mother whispered to her husband in Oberhausen prison: "we will say that we were only offered shares…but did not buy any." My father could not have visited my mother in Oberhausen, because he himself was in Halle at the time, hundreds of miles away. It cannot even be established whether he knew that Oberhausen was the place where she'd been taken into custody. Heinrich L continued:

"Strauss suggested that while I was being moved from Halle to Hanover I should try to escape by giving the accompanying officer a hook to the chin. Then I should make a dash for it so that I could contact his friend "F" to warn him to leave the country immediately."

Indeed, my father had a good friend and business partner whose name began with an F.

Had my father, in desperation, asked a fellow prisoner for help to warn his friend to leave Germany or had the Nazis simply invented Heinrich L's story? I favored invention, until I read on:

"After I had made contact with F, I was to tell him he should give me 50RM and ask him to take me with him across the border, if possible. Once abroad, Strauss said, F would take care of my progress because he was a 'very fine person,' I would see that for myself."

This last piece of so-called evidence had a ring of authenticity about it. It recalled the devastation my father expressed about F's untimely passing in one of his letters to my mother. In this letter, he compared the impact of losing F to that of his mother's death. Was this one of the "acts of desperation," which later, he himself found hard to credit, that kept returning to the forefront of my mind?

"Strauss told me that Krause offered his uncle Gustav a political position for 1000RM a month…[he knew] their political discussions in Tetschen were being monitored…Krause gave Gustav an envelope with a lot of money in it to give to someone in Halle…Strauss said, 'Man, this is treason, for this you get the death penalty': he claimed during his interrogation he was talked into [the trip to Tetschen] by his aunt and uncle, but he told me this wasn't true, he and his uncle knew exactly what was going on, this Krause has a connection to Russia."

"Strauss predicted Communism would come and then scores would be settled with the [Nazis] and this disgusting mess in Germany would be brought to a swift conclusion…Hitler and the other top ones would be assassinated [which is what] Krause said would come at the end. Strauss said Krause would give him away which would lead the Nazis to shoot him and then all would be lost."

Heinrich L. ended his statement with a ready judgment for the Nazi court:

"I was sure from the first moment…that in the person of Strauss we had a strong opponent of National Socialism…I claim no reward or privilege for my activities in the service of explaining the matter against Strauss and did not give this statement for these reasons."

Adolf G, a bricklayer, was serving time in Halle prison for an unnamed crime. While there, he was accused of aiding and abetting my father and his uncle by passing notes back and forth between them and out of the prison. It was claimed that Adolf G helped my father smuggle two letters to his friends on the outside by passing them to a baker's apprentice who was supposed to post them, but handed them to the authorities instead. The intercepted letter my father tried to smuggle to Gustav lent some credibility to Adolf G's claims. He apparently stated that he was also prepared to assist my father and Gustav escape for a reward of 200RM which Gustav had promised he would arrange for him once they'd made a safe getaway. The details of the planned escape are not referred to. How much embellishment went into Adolf G's statements cannot be verified.

Four months after my father wrote to the Halle magistrate, he prepared the seventeen-page statement Noemi and I had seen at the Berlin Federal Archives. The court, perhaps wanting to appear legitimate, had the handwritten document typed in duplicate. One copy was to be sent to the Attorney General of the Magistrate's Court, the other was to go to the Special Witness file.

Apparently, my father's lengthy plea represented a last-ditch attempt to clear his name. He seems to have believed that if he re-told the truth in greater detail, even if that meant publicly admitting to some of his weaknesses, the court would see that they were accusing an innocent man.

To the People's Court in Berlin, 12th October 1936. A summary:

"In special measure my childhood memories are bound up with my aunt Hilde Flörsheim in whose house I spent a part of my youth. Since she cared for me and my sick mother when I was a young boy, I felt myself drawn to her. After my mother died and I was working away from home during years of inflation and trying to survive on a meager retainer, she found me accommodation with relatives which eased my money worries and also my loneliness."

"In August 1934, the first occasion on which I met Franz Krause, I told my aunt that he did not fit into the family milieu. She replied that she owed Krause her marriage since he had successfully intervened in one of her husband's illicit love affairs."

"My plans to emigrate were thwarted by my wife's pregnancy so I turned to my uncle to perform an abortion. Gustav refused but offered to take us to a Dr. Stern in Karlsbad in Czechoslovakia, on the condition that I pay him 20 Reichmarks a day for lost working time in Zeitz, which I rejected."

"I then approached the layman (in Mülheim) whose double attempt to induce an abortion in my wife resulted in a dangerous illness that led us back to Gustav. I again asked him to perform an abortion and again he refused."

"When Gustav requested my company on the drive to Tetschen his suggestion drew amusement from several other friends present. Because of my personal aversion to Krause, I initially refused, but I also did not want to leave my sick wife. Gustav then demanded that I join him in order to pay the petrol costs which would reciprocate his hospitality and medical care. He also suggested that Krause could give me some business advice about the patenting of the sign-painting device. When that, too, didn't work he began threatening in a furious rage that rose to a storm that he would break off all family relations. At this point my aunt took me aside and begged me for the sake of wedded peace to give in. She also requested that during the trip I ask Krause to talk her husband out of the idea of a position abroad."

"Evidently, my resistance was broken by this double pressure." (His aunt's supplications and his uncle's threat.) (Dieser doppelten Bedrägnis erlag schliesslich mein Widerstand).

Even in this statement my father does not attempt an explanation of the telegram he wrote at Gustav's instigation. Was he embarrassed by his own naiveté? In any event, it was one of the key issues the court used to prove his guilt. He does, however, quote his political differences with Gustav and the political conversations he had with Krause.

"Although I never in my life busied myself with politics, either actively or passively, I did stand in opposition to Flörsheim's views. He described me in the presence of others as an orphan boy, someone around whom one can run rings. When he predicts the end of National Socialism I say to him or my aunt, we will speak again in twenty or thirty years and see which of us was right and he then says to me I don't understand the game."

"Krause predicted that Fascism would receive a moral blow through Italy's loss of the war with Abyssinia. He said the German economy could not sustain itself due to the scarcity of raw materials and the investment in roads and armaments. Fewer exports would create a lack of foreign currency."

"I informed Krause that exports were on the rise and unemployment was down. As to the scarcity of raw materials, I assured him in my own area of business the storerooms were full of wool and cotton. I maintained that apart from the insignificant number of disaffected people, the enthusiasm of the German people for The Third Reich was not predicated on the material comfort of the individual. The personality of the Führer would preserve the eagerness and support of his people, despite some flaws."

"Krause dismissed all this as superficial and accused me of bias due to my reading of the German papers only. He claimed he was better at gauging the true picture and was convinced the workers were dissatisfied enough to take strike action."

"I maintained that our security forces, the SA (Storm Troopers) and SS (Secret Police) would take care to keep the peace and handle the strikes in the event of unrest. He countered this by saying I had no idea how these organizations and the German army operated, and that he did, because he had contacts at the highest levels. In fact, he foresaw a communist subversion already underway and believed that the SA and SS would join in. In reply to my question as to whether he thought violence would break out, Krause held that in a revolution anything is possible. I said I feared this scenario since it would bring with it the worst pogroms the world had seen, irrespective of the instigators."

"Krause also maintained that Germany was upsetting the peace and would start a war in Europe. I disagreed and said any government which purposefully begins a war should be removed, since the people were against such horrors."

"It was made known to me that during his interrogation my uncle claimed that taking my sign-painting device with me to show Krause was only intended as a disguise. I repeat, I know nothing about this. The first time a possible disguise was mentioned was on the return journey when my uncle said to me in the car that if I am questioned about the trip I am to say we had visited an acquaintance and demonstrated my device to him."

"In the end, I found a few minutes alone with Krause to ask him on behalf of my aunt to desist from creating senseless illusions in my uncle, since his sexual predilections would make him unsuitable for a political position. Krause replied that he'd had similar thoughts and had already been asked that by the family once before."

"Although there was absolutely no talk of my connection to politics, I described myself as unsuitable for political activity so as not to present my uncle alone as unsuitable. Krause subsequently told my uncle that although he'd tried to arrange an overseas posting for him, difficulties had arisen and he would be better off staying in his medical practice because the situation in Germany would improve through the people's rejection of anti-Semitism."

"After lunch my uncle took an envelope from Krause which I suspect contained money which he was supposed to deliver to a man in Halle unknown to me. My uncle told me this on the journey home."

"While driving back to Zeitz my uncle was very depressed and made disparaging remarks about Krause. He called him a swindler and wanted nothing more to do with him. I agreed with this late realization and once again repeated my opinion of Krause that I had previously shared with my aunt."

"I was unhappy with myself for having gone on the trip to Tetschen out of a mistaken consideration for my aunt, though I believed it had not been in vain since I convinced Krause to stop making empty promises to my uncle."

My father's essentially compliant nature was no match for his conniving uncle. Since the mercenary Gustav had extended hospitality to him, it was almost a foregone conclusion that he could talk my father into returning a favor. Even my father's obligation to his sick fiancée could not override his feelings of indebtedness to his uncle and aunt. Moreover, Gustav's threat to cut family ties, thereby denying my father access to his aunt, was a threat he would have taken very much to heart.

As for the political conversations that took place in Tetschen, with the benefit of hindsight one can judge both my father and Krause as being right and wrong on certain issues. On the face of things it seems that my father seriously misread the political situation if, in 1936, he truly believed what he had written and was not simply playing to the gallery. Nevertheless, it is interesting to speculate at which point my father "saw the light," in view of his comment to Noemi later in life that had he not been Jewish, he's not sure he'd have been able to see through Nazi propaganda.

In any event, his apparent support for the National Socialists did nothing to overturn the findings of the court.

Who was Franz Krause?

Research conducted with the assistance of the Halle Memorial revealed that when my father first met Krause, who was not Jewish, the former Social Democrat was the thirty-four year old editor of the newspaper, "Zeitzer Volksblatt," (Zeitz People's Paper).

His father was born in Czechoslovakia and came to Germany at the end of the 19th century. Franz was born in Zeitz in 1900.

Although Krause was the intermediary for the SPD and the Communist Party in his hometown, he was not a communist and did not work for the Russians, contrary to what the Gestapo believed. After he escaped from Germany, Krause lived in Czechoslovakia until early 1938, when he tried to flee to Bolivia. However, he was arrested by Italian police as he was crossing the border into Italy, charged with carrying a firearm and sentenced to twelve months imprisonment. While serving this term, he assaulted a jailer for which he received a further twenty months in prison. In August 1941, he was extradited to Germany and tried in the People's Court. Two years later, he was sent to Brandenburg-Görden prison, which held huge numbers of political prisoners and was known as the German "Sing-Sing." In 1945, he was transferred to Ichterhausen prison and it is believed from there was deported to his death.

The Supreme Court of Prussia sitting in Halle tried my father and his aunt Hilde "In the Name of the German People." Also on trial were two of their relatives and four former members of the SPD. Gustav's trial was heard in the People's Court in Berlin and the protocols do not say why.

In its summing up the court offered background summaries of the accused followed by descriptions of their real or invented transgressions against the state.

The accused, Hilde Flörsheim.

The court's findings about Hilde began with a short paragraph on Gustav, (a moody man who was casual about marital fidelity) and held that she acted under his influence. In 1926, he was charged with performing an illegal abortion that led to a conviction of eighteen months in prison and a loss of his medical license (which might explain why he refused to perform an abortion on my mother even before he recognized that her condition made it impossible). Following his deregistration as a doctor, his economic circumstances deteriorated and that situation, together with "the position that is allowed the Jews in The Third Reich," accounts for his apparent disenchantment with the National Socialist state.

The protocols state that Hilde knew of Krause's illegal work before and after his escape to Czechoslovakia, and also about her husband's illegal relationship to him, while conceding that she may not have known about the details of their activities. It was clear to her that her husband's relationship to Krause was different from that which was presented to her as a job search for him. She also passed on two letters involving a family member (one of the accused) which were sent to Krause in Tetschen. Apparently Hilde had stated that her participation in an earlier trip to Tetschen was completely innocent and that she heard none of the political discussions that took place.

"These statements of the accused are so dull that they hardly need refuting…the Supreme Court has not the slightest doubt that she observed everything and heard everything and was aware of the consequences…"

The accused, Gottfried Strauss

The contents of the five pages of the court's protocols on my father revealed some interesting information which enabled comparisons to be made between what my father purportedly said in his statements, and what his uncle had said about him.

The protocols state that my father first met Gustav as his aunt's husband when he was sixteen. He spent a lot of time at the Flörsheim's while he was an apprentice buyer in Frankfurt, "without taking particularly to his uncle-by-marriage." (Elsewhere it is stated that my father disapproved of his uncle's philandering because it made his aunt unhappy). When the Flörsheims moved to Zeitz, these many visits stopped, though good family relations continued.

Despite my father having claimed that he himself had resigned from his job in June 1935, Gustav had insisted he was sacked. Did the court accept my father's version because it cast a better light on The Third Reich?

The six-month sentence my father received for a breach of regulations controlling foreign exchange is then mentioned, without any further explanation.

The protocols proceed to address my father's knowledge of Krause. It is claimed that during my parents' visit to the Flörsheims,

Gustav told my father about Krause's anti-government activities. "In the main, Strauss denied this, but after lengthy backwards and forwards, admitted it."

At first, it seems my father was adamant, as can be seen from his letter to the Halle magistrate, that he "failed to discern either the scope or the nature of [Krause's] activities in Germany and later in the CSR [and that they] only became clear to [him] after [his] involuntary trip to Tetschen." In the end, however, the protocols stated that "Strauss then admitted that the trip to Tetschen was undertaken both for the purposes of finding a job for his uncle and in order to carry out illegal activities." That my father had claimed that he had no interest in these illegal activities was of no concern to the court and changed nothing.

Disregarding my father's detailed account of "the various circumstances which turned [his] energetic resistance to making the trip with Flörsheim into the precise opposite" (his letter to the Halle magistrate), and the same claim expressed differently in his appeal to the Peoples' Court that, "[his] resistance was broken by this double pressure of [his] aunt's supplications to intervene in Krause's job offers to her husband and his uncle's threat to cut family ties," the court described his capitulation: "After some to-ing and fro-ing it was agreed that the trip should take place and that Strauss should accompany Flörsheim." (Nach einigem Hin und Her wurde man sich einig, dass die Fahrt stattfinden und dass Strauss mitfahren sollte).

Later in the protocols, the court is prepared to recognize that "it was also the pleas of his aunt which led him to take part in the journey," though this didn't influence the final verdict.

At first, the court's account of the telegram my father wrote is favorable to his version. "At Flörsheim's request, Strauss wrote a telegram to the cover address of Wedlich in which he confirmed the arrangement. At the instigation of Flörsheim, he chose the signature 'Marianne Strauss.' Flörsheim explained that Krause would then know who the telegram was from." Yet, two pages later it is claimed that, "the defense of the accused will be disproved by the entire facts of the case and by his conduct. [He] knew Krause was working illegally, he knew Flörsheim was in contact with him and not just about obtaining a job. This was expressed in a totally unambiguous and unmistakable way by the writing of the telegram with its fictitious name...Strauss was not at all capable of giving an explanation for this cover-up."

The court's summing up of the political discussions that took place between my father, Flörsheim and Krause in Tetschen does not match either the conclusions of the investigation as written up in the Bill of Indictment 28th September 1936, or what my father reported in his interrogations and in his long statement.

In my father's first interrogation he presented the political conversations held in Tetschen as talks between Gustav and Krause, with some interjections of his, which he said had annoyed his uncle. In his long statement, however, he comes across as something of an advocate of National Socialism. The Bill of Indictment, on the other hand, claims my father said, "Adolph Hitler and the rest of the leaders must be eliminated." Yet, the Supreme Court's summing up absolved him of this by pointing the finger at the absent Krause; "Strauss asked what would then happen to the Führer and other leading personalities to which Krause replied that they would naturally have to be shot.

The discussions continued around questions of espionage, but according to Strauss, without the actual word 'spying' being used." The sign-painting device is then again referred to in a way which at first appears to support my father. "Strauss's defense rests on his claim that he only participated in the journey to negotiate the utilization of the sign-painting device...that he did not even speak to Krause about it can be explained by his realizing that he was not the right man." But then the court changed tack, claiming that the defense of the accused will be disproved because "his participation in the trip and his taking along of the sign-painting device were for purposes of disguise. This comes to light entirely unequivocally in the testimonies of the witness Irene Strauss…a proof of this is that in his conversations with Krause, Strauss did not even attempt to enter into the matter of the sign-painting device…from here it can be seen as proven that Strauss participated in the journey in order to disguise the undertaking."

The court had managed to lay a good portion of the blame for my father's conviction at the feet of my mother, and one wonders whether my parents ever discussed the issue, before the events faded into history.

The court did not refer to my father seeking a job in Russia or Czechoslovakia although he had answered a question about it in his first interrogation and had also referred to it in his long statement. As well, the Bill of Indictment had devoted five lines to the point: "Krause stated that he was director of espionage and that he had big connections at his disposal. He asked Strauss and Flörsheim to work with him on this matter promising to get them highly influential positions with good remuneration in this illegal work either in Czechoslovakia or Russia."

However, the Supreme Court ignored the issue of work abroad in its summation. Not only was it superfluous to the evidence it had already amassed, the outcome of the hearing was a foregone conclusion.

In its final verdict the court spoke of my father and his aunt Hilde together "…regarding the extent of the punishment notice was to be taken of the scope of the activity. The accused Hilde Flörsheim was a more frequent accomplice of her husband's than Strauss. But she was naturally more subjugated to his will and more dependent upon him than Strauss. The Supreme Court therefore judged both of them equally. Since, in addition to this, the consequences of the activities, in so far as could be proven are not overly serious, the case was concluded by imposing the minimum penalty of two years penitentiary for both of the accused since they, through their deeds, placed themselves outside the society to which, as Jews, they also belong. In their capacity as citizens of the German Reich they must be stripped of their civil rights for a period of three years."

Thus, even though my father's and his aunt's "crime" was considered "not overly serious" it condemned my father (and mother) to many more months of abject misery. (Hilde's prison conditions are unknown to me, though, as has been indicated, she, Gustav and their young daughter later perished in a concentration camp).

Stripping convicted prisoners of their civil rights was a risible punishment when it pertained to Jews, since by 1937, they had few left to mention.

In the criminal matter against Flörsheim and others regarding preparation for high treason, the following verdict was announced in the main hearing in front of the 5th criminal division in Halle (Saale) on 29th January 1937, with my mother and grandfather present.

"Hilde Flörsheim and Gottfried Strauss, each to two years penitentiary and three years loss of civil rights."

"In the case of the accused Hilde Flörsheim fourteen months and one week."

"In the case of Gottfried Strauss nine months and one week."

I was surprised to see a modicum of justice in the sentencing in that the period of time my father had been held in custody without bail was returned to him in the final lighter sentence. Hilde's sentence was also reduced to fourteen months and one week which might have indicated that she had been remanded in custody for almost ten months before the trial. But I saw no evidence of her stay in prison.

Inconsistencies in the dispensing of Nazi law remained right up to the outbreak of war, growing steadily worse until there was nothing left of the law's independence from the murderous political decrees that the Nazis passed and the court rubber-stamped.

It still amazes me that this Kafkaesque chapter of my parents' past is stored for posterity in the archives of their homeland.

I wonder whether, over the years, they ever thought about the files that the Nazis had amassed on them. My guess is they did not. With Germany's defeat in the war and the universal discrediting and condemnation of The Third Reich, they may never have given the paperwork compiled on their interrogations another thought. But, who knows?

The grandfather who stirred my interest when my father first mentioned him in an early letter from Halle rarely missed a mention thereafter in my parents' correspondence. Thus, it soon became obvious that Karl Strauss and my parents shared a special bond enabling them to support one another throughout the years of my father's incarceration. Nowhere is their mutual affection better expressed than in my father's following lines:

Halle, 3rd May 1936

Dear Father also wrote me he is in positive raptures about you and every word comes straight from the heart, just as you feel about him. He's the best person I know...and his future depends on us.

Towards the end of my father's sentence Karl's appearance at the prison, and his subsequent letter to the authorities requesting a suspension of further imprisonment and parole, was in keeping with my father's description. And, after he himself became a prisoner of the Nazis, his words from Amberg penitentiary–"may the Good Lord see to it that everything you and yours wish for themselves comes true since your well-being is of special comfort to me"–aroused my love and admiration of him. At the same time it also greatly saddened me since, had it not been for Hitler and the Nazis, we'd surely have known one another.

The future for which my parents felt responsible took a dramatic turn for the worse on Kristallnacht, according to documents Facts and Files retrieved from five different archives in northern Bavaria, including the records of the Bayreuth District Court. But my grandfather had also suffered his fair share of hardships before Hitler's rise to power.

Karl Strauss was born in Hollfeld Kreis, Bavaria, on 5th May 1873 to Joseph Strauss and Cecilie Kohn whose first son, Sigmund, had been born the year before. At the beginning of the twentieth century the family moved to the Bavarian city of Kulmbach. Nothing is known to me about my grandfather's childhood prior to 1894 when, at the age of twenty one, he reported for military duty and served for three years in the First Bavarian Regiment of Horse Cavalry at Bamberg and with the Third (Horse) Squadron of the Bavarian Artillery Company at Nüremberg. In 1905, in his early thirties, he married Frieda Hamburger in Würzburg. Frieda, whose photo adorns a wall in my study, was a pretty woman eleven years Karl's junior. Gottfried, the couple's only child, was born two years later.

Karl and Frieda enjoyed a happy marriage until Frieda contracted consumption. After a long and painful struggle with the disease she died at age thirty-nine. Karl did not re-marry.

When World War I broke out in 1914, my grandfather fought for his country, and at the end of hostilities was discharged with the rank of Lance Corporal and awarded the standard third class medal for combat soldiers.

For a time, it seems, Karl joined the family business, Joseph Strauss and Sons, which dealt in the horse and cattle trade. Whether this was his first choice for making a living, or whether it was expected of him to follow in his brother's and father's footsteps, is unknown.

Judging from letters my grandfather wrote his son between 1926 and 1933, Karl at some point apparently started his own business and was constantly striving to balance the books. Repayments of bank loans, mortgages and spiraling interest rates aggravated by galloping inflation proved an ever-present worry. From numerous mentions of percentages, sureties, debtors and creditors, it appeared money was always in short supply and business was often "lousy." However, what impressed me about this small collection of letters which, by and large, relate to economic matters, was the trust my grandfather placed in the financial savvy of his nineteen-year-old son. My father, at the time, was a successful apprentice buyer in a large retail firm. Not only was the younger man able to offer his father business advice he also pledged monetary assistance. Acknowledging this, my grandfather wrote:

Kulmbach, 15th January 1933

"…I knew that you would help me financially. Nevertheless, 1000Mark is not much in the livestock trade and I will not and cannot ask that you invest more."

To further ease his pecuniary constraints in 1932 my grandfather sublet rooms in his apartment to a non-Jewish couple, Ida and Hans Weber; in return Frau Weber kept house for him for which he paid her 47RM per month.

It seems Karl had needed help to run his domestic affairs ever since his wife's death, and apparently he was quite adamant that potential employees fit into the family milieu. One of the women who worked for him before Frau Weber was employed because she was well educated, and "would get on splendidly with Grandmother."

Evidently, the arrangement with the Webers suited both parties since it lasted several years even after Nazi legislation made their co-habitation problematic.

The infamous 1935 Nüremberg Laws, which formed the corner-stones of Nazi racial policy, encouraged Germans to distance themselves from their Jewish neighbors. In addition to prohibiting marriage and sexual relations between Jews and Aryans, the legis-lation stated that Jews were forbidden from employing German maids under the age of forty-five. Since Frau Weber was thirty-eight when she and her husband moved in with my grandfather (her date of birth was noted on several archival documents found by Facts and Files) she was, in fact, ineligible for employment. But, as he employed her before the racist law was passed they all went on as before.

Despite sharing his living quarters to help pay the rent, my grand-father's financial situation deteriorated further. In 1935, according to communications he conducted with the tax office, Karl became dependent on my father for clothing and underwear. In a letter to the Finance Office in Kulmbach, dated 16th March 1936, he stated: "Without the support of my relatives I would not have been able to maintain my already Spartan lifestyle."

One of Karl's nephews, Eric Strauss, according to records, helped him during 1936, by sending him a monthly stipend amounting to 610RM, a not inconsiderable sum. This impressive generosity was a kind of repayment for the fact that my father had bailed his cousin Eric out of bankruptcy some years before.

By November 1937, my grandfather could no longer maintain the apartment he'd shared with Ida and Hans Weber. The couple found themselves new living quarters while Karl moved in with his brother Sigmund where Frau Weber continued to help out with housekeeping. Karl stayed with his brother for ten months until Sigmund lost the lease on his place obliging my grandfather to find alternative accommodation. As it happened, in September 1938, the Webers invited him to re-join them at their new address and my grandfather accepted.

In March of that year, Karl had applied for and received social welfare benefits, and by May had been forced to de-register his business due to the Nazi take-over of Jewish enterprises. He subsequently registered as a trader in oils and fats after which his social welfare payments ceased. His annual profits had fallen from 1,100RM in 1933 to 72RM at the end of 1937. By June 1938 he was nearly 3,700RM in debt which somehow did not prevent him from sending money orders (that might have been borrowed from his own father or other relatives) to my father in concentration camp.

1938 was a watershed year for the Jews of Germany; for my grandfather, the events in the wake of Kristallnacht were beyond imagining. As already indicated, Facts and Files established that he was, indeed, one of the Jews taken into temporary protective custody on 10th November, and shortly after, placed in a cell in the court prison of Kulmbach, the same prison in which my father was held for five hours on his way to Dachau. This, then, was his location when my father in Buchenwald began to suspect my mother of "keeping [him] in the dark" about his father's well-being.

However, the massive, nationwide anti-Semitic assault during the night of 9th to 10th November need not necessarily have prevented my grandfather's release and emigration with my parents a few months later. Karl's brother Sigmund, who had been arrested at the same time as Karl, was released and somehow managed to flee to the US. However, for Karl, the Night of the Shattered Glass temporarily obscured a far more serious move that was secretly underway to ensnare him.

The widespread fear and unrest the massacre created led the Criminal Investigation Department in Kulmbach, on 12th November, to release an official statement "explaining" its actions to the Jews of the city.

"In consequence of the death of the German ambassadorial official in Paris, Ernest Vom Rath, who has been treacherously murdered by a Jew, the local population has been gripped by considerable agitation. All manner of utterances have been made in condemnation of this despicable crime, which caused the authorities to fear for the safety of the local Jews."

This wickedly ambiguous message proved to be the justification for the CID's arrest of the city's Jewish men including the Strauss brothers.

Kulmbach had been a National Socialist stronghold for many years before Hitler came to power, though anti-Semitic incidents up to 1933 had been limited to verbal abuse and swastika scrawling. However, in March 1933, the Bavarian Ministry of Justice was taken over by a thirty-two year old Nazi activist, Hans Frank, who belonged to a secret anti-Semitic group. Though his political influence was limited, he continued to advance his vision for the Nazi legal system coining the phrase: "Justice is whatever is useful for the German people," often cited as the epitome of the Nazi disdain for the law.

Nine days after Kristallnacht, the Lord Mayor of Kulmbach announced that the "justified indignation" against Kulmbach's Jews had calmed down to the point where he felt it was safe to order the release of my grandfather. However, the intended move did not go according to plan. A superintendent of the Criminal Investigation Department received instructions to hold him while an investigation was carried out on his business accounts, purportedly suspected of containing irregularities. Yet, the scores of pages of my grandfather's book-keeping and bank statements found in the Bamberg Archives show that every ingoing and outgoing Reichmark was painstakingly accounted for. Not surprisingly, the investigation was a ruse. Thus, the local Nazi party leadership brought to the prosecutor's office in Bayreuth the charge they had been waiting to bring for some time.

The arrest order from the County Court, Kulmbach, to the Chief Prosecutor in Bayreuth, drew on the legal precepts of the Nüremberg Laws:

"Karl Strauss…is under suspicion of having, since 1933 until 1938 inclusive, contravened paragraph 2 of the Law for the Protection of German Blood and Honor of 15th September 1935 constituting a criminal offence according to paragraph 5, section 2 of the said law. The arrest has been ordered because a criminal offence is the object of the investigation and the suspect might flee the country…furthermore it would not be tolerated in the eyes of the public to set the accused free. Viz paragraph 122, sections 1 and 2 of the State police (Gestapo)."

An anonymous informer involved in my grandfather's denunciation had written a note to the relevant Nazi party members and signed it, "An enemy of the Jews."

As I had learned from Frank Drauschke at Facts and Files, and later saw for myself in history books and in the protocols of my father's trial, informers worked everywhere throughout The Third Reich and it seems my grandfather was yet another of their victims.

When I noticed from the research that the non-Jewish Ida Weber was arrested two days after my grandfather, the pieces of the puzzle began falling into place, revealing the nature of my grandfather's "criminal offence." It also shed light on the conversation my parents had had with Sigmund's sons in the US in 1971 concerning the "Aryan matter" and Karl's mention of the same issue in his letter from Amberg prison.

My grandfather was accused of committing race defilement by having had sex with his trusted house-keeper, a criminal offence under Nazi law. Frau Weber, on the other hand, an Aryan female, could not be charged with this crime–despite being arrested–and probably had more to fear from her cuckolded husband.

In any event, both were interrogated and fingerprinted. I was intrigued to see that the prison had also noted my grandfather's physical characteristics though, regrettably, I couldn't recognize any of my own features in the cold listing of those belonging to the relative I supposedly resembled; forehead: broad; nose: long; mouth: ordinary; chin: round; facial shape: broad; build: stocky. Interestingly, though, we were both 175 centimeters tall.

If my grandfather was interrogated before Frau Weber, and it seems from later remarks by the judges that he was, the protocols found by Facts and Files do not include this prior interrogation. The material, as arranged in the dossier by F&F, presents Ida Weber's statement first, followed by my grandfather's response to it.

"After initial denials, the accused Ida Weber made the following statement":

"On 15th April 1915 I married Hans Weber…we lived in Leipzig and were quite happy…in November 1916 we relocated to Kulmbach and lived with my parents-in-law for about sixteen years. Because we couldn't find alternative accommodation, we moved into the apartment of Karl Strauss as sub-tenants on 1st October 1932."

"Soon after moving in with him he began propositioning me. This happened whenever my husband was away working as a commercial traveler. I tried to resist him but eventually we had sexual intercourse…every four to eight weeks…we continued this while he was living with his brother…the last time would have been about two weeks ago."

"[Strauss] was known to be a decent person…"

Referring to the time Karl moved in with the Webers she says:

"Other Jewish persons never came to our place. My husband never had any dealings with Jews."

Ida and Hans Weber were not members of the Nazi party though they supported the NSV (National Socialist Peoples' Welfare) and the DAF (German Labor Front).

"I knew I was not supposed to have sexual relations with a Jew after the Nüremberg Laws were promulgated but despite this I allowed myself to be seduced."

My grandfather and Ida Weber began their affair about three years before the iniquitous laws were passed but, it seems, could not overcome their natural inclinations despite being aware of the dangers involved.

"The Jew Strauss always kissed me during sexual intercourse…I was totally captivated by him and could not help myself…other than having sexual intercourse, he and I have not committed any indecent acts…my husband has, to this day, not the slightest inkling of the affair between myself and Strauss…I often told Strauss my husband would kill me if he found out but the Jew had no sensitivities in this regard, he cared only for his own satisfaction."

"As a girl I led a decent and virtuous life and was a virgin when I married my husband. It was only the Jew Karl Strauss who abused me sexually in this despicable manner. I now bitterly regret what happened. It would never have come to this had the Jew Strauss not been so persistent. When I did not want to do it, he would force me to have sex. He would grab me and put me down on the bed."

"The information I have given here is the absolute truth and I have nothing further to add…I have no reason to protect the Jew any further. In the interests of protecting my name and that of my child, I plead for mitigating circumstances in this matter."

When Ida and Hans Weber first joined my grandfather they did so as a childless couple after a marriage of seventeen years. Eight and a half months after moving in with him Ida gave birth to a baby girl. She states:

"I cannot say with absolute certainty who the father of my child is, whether it is the Jew Strauss or my husband…as far as I know Strauss always wore a condom when we had intercourse because I always worried something might happen."

It was to be expected that the forced public accounting of a private, long-standing and possibly caring relationship, would turn into something else once it was judged to be a crime. Ida Weber herself couldn't decide whether Karl Strauss had taken advantage of her or whether she willingly participated in sexual activities with the man she claimed captivated her. If she now spoke of him with almost total disrespect she was driven by fear of the consequences.

Before my grandfather spoke, Ida Weber's testimony, which appears to be twice as long as his, was read out to him:

"I have just been made aware of the statement made by Frau Weber which, by and large, corresponds to the actual facts. I would, however, categorically deny that I ever, when having sexual intercourse with her, used force…even on the first occasion, she agreed to have sex with me without offering the slightest objection. She never resisted, on the contrary she complained to me that her husband did not have sex with her for long periods of time and often came home late and drunken…we did not have sexual intercourse during her pregnancy…I always wore condoms… therefore I cannot be considered to be the father of the now five-and-a-half year old girl of the Webers."

"I was well aware that, under the Nüremberg Laws, I was forbidden from having sexual relations with an Aryan woman, but gave in because the opportunity was there; besides, Frau Weber was always more than ready because of her husband's apparent disinterest. For myself I gained little enjoyment of it, for reasons of my age-related reduced capacity."

The true nature of the relationship between my grandfather and Ida Weber prior to their arrest will always belong to them alone. Yet Karl's attempt to disassociate himself from the pleasure he derived from it is poignant in the extreme.

Ida's husband Hans Weber claimed his marriage had been happy at all times, that there had been no major disagreements between him and his wife, and insisted he had been totally ignorant of the affair between her and "the Jew Strauss," presumably until the trial. He did concede, however, that he had reproached his wife repeatedly because "she fussed over Strauss too much and took great trouble over his linen etc." This comment seems to indicate that, despite her less than flattering remarks about Karl in her testimony, Ida Weber wanted to please her lover.

In further questioning, Frau Weber stated that until she was arrested, her married life had been harmonious. She admitted there were occasions when her husband would arrive home at a somewhat late hour because of his job. As well, she said, he may have been a little tipsy now and then but never had there been major quarrels. She confessed to minor disagreements from time to time, which she claimed occurred in all marriages but it didn't follow that the marriage was unhappy.

It seems Ida saw no contradiction between her so-called happy marriage and her affair with my grandfather.

As in the matter of my parents' interrogations, what each party actually said, and what was taken down by the Nazis, may not always have been one and the same thing. Facts and Files even suspected the Nazis of inventing my grandfather's affair in order to keep him in jail after Kristallnacht. Matthias suggested the opportunity to accuse him of being a "criminal Jew," and prosecute him in a show trial, was too good to pass up, and that his and Ida Weber's confessions were possibly made under extreme pressure.

If Facts and Files are right, which in this instance only I tend to doubt, Karl's reference to the "Aryan" matter in his letter from Amberg and my parents' discussion of the subject with Karl's nephews in the US in my absent-minded presence, may yet have referred to trumped-up charges. That the Nazis exploited the issue for a show trial, however, seems to have been the case.

After prying into the bedroom activities of Karl Strauss and Ida Weber in order to enforce a racist law, the court ordered that documentation be found to prove that my grandfather's maternal and paternal parents were Jews. In 1935, the Nazis defined a Jew as one who had three or four Jewish grandparents or belonged to a Jewish religious community. Karl, as far as I know qualified on both accounts.

Nevertheless, driven by the need to demonstrate that the laws were being carried out to the letter, Kulmbach's mayor led the search for the relevant documents.

He wrote to his counterpart in Hollfeld on 22nd November 1938, requesting Karl's birth certificate, his parents' birth and marriage certificates and those of his maternal and paternal grandparents. Difficulties arose because the official register of births and deaths in Hollfeld was begun only in 1876, three years after Karl was born. Not to be deterred, the Mayor instructed his officers to contact the Jewish authorities in surrounding districts. An approach was made to the rabbinical offices in Bamberg where Karl was a member of the synagogue in order to obtain marriage certificates of his parents but ironically, the Rabbi was in protective custody, doubtlessly having been arrested during Kristallnacht. Nevertheless, his whereabouts were located and he was obliged to make a statement:

"The accused Karl Strauss is known to me personally…the Strauss family has been recorded as living in Heiligenstadt since the year 1700 and, as far as I know, worked in the butcher's trade. One of the family living in Hollfeld told me that he led a rather loose life and was considered to be a somewhat unreliable person."

Perhaps, only the promise of a release from custody could have persuaded the Rabbi to besmirch the reputation of a fellow Jew in such dangerous times.

In any event, further written enquiries about my grandfather's background were made on 30th January 1939 at the Gestapo headquarters in Nüremberg. A reply from Nüremberg stating that relevant documents were to be found in the rabbinical offices in Regensburg was sent to the Bayreuth Prosecutor's office because about two months earlier Karl had been moved by mass transport to Bayreuth's county court jail. The Regensburg documents, however, were not found and on 17th February 1939, the Bayreuth county court informed the Gestapo that determining the Jewish descent of Karl Strauss was still encountering considerable difficulties.

Finally, at the registry office in Bayreuth, papers were found proving that Karl's mother and father and grandparents on both sides were Jews.

Why the fascist dictatorship went to such extraordinary lengths to determine Jewish heritage puzzled me until I found a plausible explanation in Nikolaus Wachsmann's book:

"…the legal system [was] a way to mask the terrorist nature of the Nazi regime [and] to secure the support of many Germans, who had long placed a great deal of importance on the maintenance of law and order."

The effort invested in trying to prove my grandfather's Jewish origins had, indeed, been immense and yet its documentation was surprisingly sloppy. Sometimes names were spelled three different ways within the space of a few pages; there were other spelling mistakes and two different dates of birth listed for my grandfather, though the records ultimately adopted the correct one known to our family.

Possibly, in an attempt to display a Nazi version of evenhandedness, the Mayor of Kulmbach also wrote to the Evangelical Church in Gröst, Querfurt, requesting the birth and marriage certificates of Ida Weber's parents and grandparents. The point of the exercise was to ensure she had no Jewish ancestors and was therefore from pure Aryan stock. The Minister of the church replied that not all documents could be found. Despite the incomplete investigation it seems the matter was not raised again by the court.

The Bayreuth county court also tried to frame my grandfather for having sex with his Aryan book-keeper, a Frau Hain, who had worked in the Strauss family business for over twenty years. Once again "an enemy of the Jews" had brought the accusation to the attention of the authorities though it is unknown whether it was the same "enemy" who denounced my grandfather earlier. In any case, the court subsequently dropped the charges after both parties categorically denied the allegations.

The hearing opened on 17th February 1939, just days, we believe, before my parents left for Shanghai. Sigmund was no longer in the country though the protocols don't mention the date of his emigration. Apart from his defense lawyer, Karl, it seems, had no other form of support since organizations which had previously assisted Jewish prisoners had been closed down by the Reich Ministry of Justice after the November 1938 pogrom.

Implementing a humiliating law which had come into force on 1st January 1939 requiring the name Sarah, for women, and Israel, for men, to be used as middle names on all Jewish documentation, the County Court of Bayreuth thus referred to my grandfather as Karl Israel Strauss. The paperwork shows, however, that its use of this official nomenclature was far from consistent.

The proceedings began by calling for character witnesses to testify on behalf of Ida Weber. The court's intention was to "ascertain the moral reputation of Frau Ida Weber and also to establish whether or not the marriage of Herr and Frau Weber could be considered a happy one."

Of course, the description of the marriage, or whether Ida was a virtuous or wanton woman, was irrelevant to the outcome of the trial since one of the aims of the case was to demonstrate the consequences, principally for Jews, of disobeying a racist edict. However, if Ida could be made to appear respectable my grandfather would be cast in an even worse light than he already was.

No fewer than eight witnesses, including her mother-in-law, a neighbor and a former employer, appeared for Ida and spoke of her in glowing terms.

Frau Weber senior claimed that Ida "was a good wife to my son at all times; she was very industrious and proper and impressed me as a thoroughly competent housewife. When I heard that she had had a sexual relationship with the Jew Karl Strauss, I was simply speechless. Such conduct is in complete contradiction to her former character."

A neighbor stated that "her household is looked after impeccably, and the cleanliness of her linen is superb. I would give her top marks."

This witness also testified that the Webers were happily married.

A previous employer reported that Ida came to her when she was very young. After she left to marry Hans, her husband had said they would be hard pressed to find another girl as good as her. "I repeat" she said, "I can give her nothing but the highest praise."

A further statement was taken from the Webers themselves who, not surprisingly, reported on their happy union.

The trial took place on 15th March 1939, in a public sitting of the Grand Criminal Division of the County Court of Bayreuth. Presiding were the president of the court and seven other legal officials. The representative of the Prosecutor's office requested that the public be excluded from the hearing until the verdict was handed down, in order to avoid corrupting public morals. However, by order of the court which undoubtedly recognized the benefits of an open trial, the request was refused, "as danger to public morality is not evident."

Due to the state of his finances Karl was represented by a defense counsel funded by legal aid.

At some point in the proceedings an astonishing–and probably mocking–piece of evidence was apparently presented by my grandfather. The protocols refer to it in the following way:

"The accused has, as he freely admitted during the hearing, always felt himself to be a full Jew…now, suddenly, in the course of the main hearing he is claiming, albeit with great inner uncertainty that, only a few weeks ago, his brother Sigmund Strauss who has emigrated, informed him that he, Karl Israel Strauss is the child of an [Aryan] shepherd with whom his mother had extra-marital relations. Most remarkable is that a fact of such importance for this case was not immediately communicated to the Criminal Division authorities and only now is brought into play at a point in time when there is no possibility to interview his brother. This kind of conduct by the accused gives the impression that his claim is utterly untrue. In addition, he let it be known that he does not care whether or not the matter is investigated."

I suspect that Sigmund, Karl's brother, was attempting to help him, long-distance, by claiming that Karl was only a half-Jew (and half Aryan). He might have known that mixed marriages, or in Karl's mother's case, mixed unions (Aryans and Jews) stood a better chance of surviving the Nazi era. The irony is that according to Orthodox Jewish law, Jewishness is passed down through the mother, though I'm certain the Nazis were disinterested in conducting their persecution of Jews according to Jewish law.

I couldn't help wondering, though, that if Karl did, indeed, have a non-Jewish father, some non-Jewish German genes may have been passed down through my father to me and might possibly account for my apparently non-Jewish appearance that is often commented upon by other Jews meeting me for the first time.

In any event, on 15th March 1939, having heard all the evidence which included the observation that my grandfather did not "terminate the relationship…when it became a punishable offence under the Nüremberg Laws," Karl Israel Strauss, without his closest family present to offer support and comfort, was found guilty of "the continuous crime of miscegenation." The court demanded a severe punishment since "it must be atonement for the long-lasting, grave injury to the highest goods of German National Community, Blood and Honor, and, at the same time, if possible, be a lesson to others who have indulged in the same crime."

He was, therefore, sentenced to ten years penitentiary with ten years loss of citizen's rights and ordered to pay costs. The defense council and the accused pleaded for utmost leniency. The sentence was reduced to eight years in penitentiary (with no apparent explanation) with three months of penal confinement to be deducted for time spent in remand, and citizen's rights were to be stripped for "only" five years.

My grandfather was ordered to remain in prison because "the reasons for his imprisonment continue to exist." The Court also referred to my grandfather's war medals:

"Because of the indecent mindset evidenced by his deeds, he can no longer be considered worthy of these decorations."

Two days after the trial Karl sent a postcard to his defense counsel instructing him to lodge an appeal. But, it is claimed, the card did not arrive and therefore his lawyer "did not take the steps [Karl] had asked him to take." Thus, on 2nd April Karl wrote to the court requesting permission to lodge a new appeal, arguing that the original deadline had been exceeded through no fault of his own. While the protocols contain no official letter of refusal the answer was clear. On 4th April Karl signed a document revoking his letter of 2nd April.

Had my grandfather completed his sentence it would have terminated on 21st December 1946, nine months after the end of the war. He could not know that long before that date, catastrophic events would lead to his own death and to the death of millions of other Jews.

Before the case was closed the chief state prosecutor in Bayreuth wrote to the county court of Kulmbach:

"Of first importance is that we recover costs of Karl Strauss's incarceration which have not nearly been offset by his impounded bank accounts."

The sum total of monies expended on my grandfather's case amounted to 3,130.85RM of which 1,977.37RM were collected from his total assets. The remaining outstanding amount was to be written-off as the debtor was now "totally without means."

Though not entirely without precedent, it is extremely rare for courts to demand from prisoners fees expended on their trial and imprisonment; the Nazi system of justice was a law unto itself.

Karl's sentence began on 22nd March 1939, a week after the trial. On the other side of the world, my parents had just arrived in Shanghai. It took another nineteen days before he was transferred to Amberg penitentiary, well known as an institution for first-time or special offenders like Jews accused of race defilement (Rassenschande). At last, the time between my parents' departure from Germany, and Karl's arrival at Amberg, was accounted for. After his imprisonment at Amberg, until his eventual arrival at Auschwitz, dates, places and times of confinement present a very confusing picture.

Although it is not possible to know what my grandfather experienced personally, historian Nikolaus Wachsmann's descriptions of Nazi prisons from 1939 to the end of the war give a general account of prisoner conditions.

He writes: "In January 1940, The Reich Ministry for Food and Agriculture decided, despite the hard physical labor expected of them, that prisoners would receive significantly less meat, fat and flour than the general population…vegetables were particularly scarce and there were severe shortages of potatoes…in some cases prisoners lost twenty kilos and more. Chronic malnutrition caused illnesses and epidemics which were exacerbated by extreme overcrowding. Medical facilities were in short supply and the treatment of ill prisoners [was] characterized by neglect and brutality."

Understandably, Karl's letter from Amberg conveyed none of this, even had he wanted to.

It is cold comfort to read that, "during the war the conditions in concentration camps (even excluding death camps) remained significantly worse than in penal institutions."

My grandfather remained in Amberg penitentiary for over two years before being transferred to Zweibrücken prison in the same administrative region. There is no reason given for the move though, apparently, it was not unusual to move prisoners around to fill labor requirements or to ease overcrowding.

By the end of 1941, the German army had begun encountering major difficulties in its invasion of the Soviet Union. The Nazi leadership had fatally underestimated the resistance put up by the Soviets resulting in almost 750,000 German casualties. This military situation had a direct impact on conditions inside Germany. In an effort to deflect attention from its huge losses, "Hitler argued that the extermination of hardened criminals, 'a-socials' and political enemies at home was a necessity as 'the best' German men were dying at the front."

Though Jewish prisoners were not specifically mentioned in this proclamation, before the following year's end, the worst would befall them.

By March 1942, Nikolaus Wachsmann claims that officials in the Reich Ministry of Justice knew that the regime had decided on the extermination of the Jews since the "final solution" to the Jewish question had been discussed in a grand Berlin villa at the Wannsee Conference two months earlier. In April, a directive from the Berlin Gestapo instructed that all Jewish prisoners were to be directly handed over to them. Those Jews still remaining in penal institutions became victims of the general transfer from autumn 1942. They had begun their journey to Auschwitz "but the true destination of the transfer remained unclear to many prisoners."

"On the day of their transfer, the prisoners were dressed in their old civilian clothes. Some particularly cruel prison officials used these last moments to taunt the prisoners, telling them that they were on their way to a place 'from where nobody returns'." Relatives were not informed of the move and in any event, my grandfather's closest family had left the country.

The prisoners were picked up by police officials who informed the local prison authorities which concentration camp their former inmates would be taken to.

However, it appears the Nüremberg and Saabrücken Gestapo, the Bayreuth Prosecutor's office and the Zweibrücken penitentiary encountered communication problems regarding the whereabouts of my grandfather.

After serving two years of his sentence at Amberg, a document shows that on 21st June 1941, my grandfather was "taken in" to Zweibrücken prison although a separate memo states that he was already "transferred" there on 12th June 1941. Could it have taken nine days to process his arrival?

Despite the Nazis' obsession with correctly detailed documentation, the records from Zweibrücken onwards offer differing accounts of the last years of his life.

On 7th October 1943, the Bayreuth Prosecutor's Office wrote to Zweibrücken penitentiary asking whether "the Jew Karl Israel Strauss" was still an inmate there and, if he was, they wanted to know when he would be handed over to the Gestapo. Two weeks later Zweibrücken informed Bayreuth that the Saarbrücken Gestapo had already collected Karl Strauss in June 1943. More than two months passed before the Bayreuth Prosecutor's Office wrote to the Saarbrücken Gestapo on 14th December 1943, complaining that it had not received "the obligatory communication concerning the Jew Strauss." Eight weeks later on 15th February 1944, a memo from the Nüremberg Gestapo to the Bayreuth Prosecutor's Office stated :

"The Jew Karl Israel Strauss was, on 2nd December 1942, taken into protective custody here as an anti-social prisoner and transferred to the concentration camp Auschwitz where he is still located. No date for his release from concentration camp has been set."

The documentation suggests that my grandfather was taken into protective custody by the Nüremberg Gestapo on 2nd December 1942, relocated to Auschwitz and again collected from there by the Saarbrücken Gestapo six months later (on 29th June 1943). While this is highly improbable because Auschwitz was the end of the road, researchers from Yad Vashem maintain that every conceivable arbitrary move made by the Nazis must be considered a likelihood until conclusive proof is established to the contrary.

The Nüremberg Gestapo memo indicates that my grandfather was still alive on 15th February 1944.

In 2014, during a visit to Australia, I was told that the International Tracing Service at Bad Arolsen had further opened up its archives to the public resulting in a huge volume of information becoming available that hadn't been when I began my enquiries regarding Karl Strauss in 1991. In addition, a friend and author of "Stolen Legacy, Nazi Theft and the Quest for Justice at Krausenstrasse 17/18, Berlin," Dina Gold, kindly offered some hitherto unknown to me contacts she'd come across in her own research.

Early in 2015, in a letter from the International Tracing Service, I received a copy of a document confirming that Karl Strauss was arrested in the Police Prison of Frankfurt on Main on 30th April 1943 and transported to Auschwitz on 10th May 1943. This information I had first received from the ITS in March 2000, but without an actual copy of the document. Subsequent research had filled in many more details of Karl Strauss's persecution before he was finally dispatched to Auschwitz.

The Nazis destroyed their documentation of the genocide of the Jews at Auschwitz before the Allies could retrieve it. Although many Jews survived the hell of this notorious death camp and were able to give testimonies of their suffering, my grandfather was not one of them.

Before my grandfather was tried and sentenced and while he was being held in one section of the County Court prison of Kulmbach, Ida Weber was being held in another. She had spent the day and night of 12th November being questioned, and the following day was released.

Awaiting her at the gates of the prison was an angry crowd of four or five hundred people including representatives of Hitler Youth, the Association of German Girls and an escort of six local Gestapo officers who forced her to parade in the main streets of the city. A placard was hung around her neck displaying a mortifying confession: "I, swine, forgetting my race, have been committing miscegenation for years until now with the Jew Karl Strauss." Frau Weber was pelted with rotten tomatoes, apples and bananas which had been distributed before the spectacle began while a member of the SA music corps played a trombone to entertain the crowd. After about half an hour she was rescued by a police lieutenant who arrived to put an end to the "entertainment." Ida Weber was returned to prison where she was held in custody for a further six weeks before being allowed to go home for Christmas.

Not surprisingly, given the salaciousness of the story, there was a photographer on hand to take a snapshot of Ida Weber surrounded by SS men, with the crowd in the background. The word "pig" (Schwein) and my grandfather's name and religion (Jude Karl Strauss), are clearly decipherable on her placard. Though the black and white photo is old, the definition of light and shade evinces the pain and ignominy on Frau Weber's downcast face.

The following day, the two Kulmbach dailies carried the story. The Bayerische Rundschau's headlines read, "Strauss, the racial defiler." The Kulmbacher Tageblatt ran the saga over three columns with the heading "Whoever does not wish to obey, must feel the consequences. A woman, forgetting her kind, was denounced because of race defilement."

From Kulmbach, the photo was flashed on the wire services of the world's newspapers and from there it eventually entered the collections of Holocaust museums in other countries, including Jerusalem's Yad Vashem.

Since becoming aware of the incident I have wondered whether my mother, still in Germany at this time, saw the photo of Frau Weber in her morning newspaper and have tried to put myself in her shoes as she suddenly recognized her father-in-law's housekeeper and his name on the placard. Though I suspect the news of my grandfather's arrest would have reached her soon after the November 1938 pogrom, she may only have learned of his appalling humiliation from the article in the newspaper.

The 1935 Nüremberg Laws on Racial Purity posed a problem of immense proportions to Jews and non-Jews alike not least because of generations of assimilation and intermarriage. However, in my grandfather's case there can be no meaningful comparison between his suffering, and that of Frau Weber's, since he paid for his "sins" with his life, whereas his "partner in crime" escaped with her life, if not her pride, intact.

I don't know how much my father learned about Karl's court case and his subsequent imprisonment after Amberg. However, I do know from documents found in my mother's apartment, that after the war when the Nüremberg Laws for the Protection of German Blood and Honor were formally revoked, my father applied for and received from Germany in 1956, a copy of the certificate of revocation.

The official certificate from the State Prosecutor's office in

Bayreuth stated:

"According to paragraph 2d 9 of the Recompensation Act to compensate for National Socialist inflicted unlawful applications of criminal legislation dated 28th May 1946, the above verdict is revoked."

At the time, our family had been living in Australia for nine years, and my grandfather had been dead for about thirteen.

By the time my parents said their farewells to my grandparents, towards the end of February 1939, Shanghai was part of their vocabulary. What I wouldn't give to know the very moment my mother and/or father realized their lives depended on getting out of Germany as swiftly as possible. Alas, this is one more answer lost to history.

In any event, as early as October 1938, my father had mentioned Shanghai in one of his letters from Buchenwald. Whether it was in response to my mother's suggestion as a possible place of refuge, or whether he had heard it from the steady stream of new inmates who brought information into the camps, is not known. Either way, my parents seemed to know that Shanghai was an open port, accepting stateless Jewish refugees, and that the Lloyd Triestino Shipping Line's vessels left regularly from Italy for the Far East. Hence, my mother purchased tickets for two second-class bunks on the MS Victoria for a passage to China, their tickets to freedom, which also demonstrated to the Gestapo their firm intention to leave. That she managed to buy the tickets was quite a feat; the availability of bunks was diminishing as an ever-increasing number of desperate Jews wanting to escape the escalating Nazi terror after Kristallnacht rushed to buy them, and prices skyrocketed.

The route my parents and their escorts–my mother once told me there were friendly Nazis–took out of the country and where they crossed the border is unknown. Many Jews fleeing Germany took a train over the Brenner Pass, the last Nazi checkpoint in the south before entering Italy. My parents, however, may have entered the Netherlands and traveled via Belgium, France and Switzerland before arriving in the north-west of Italy, and moving on to the port of Genoa where they boarded the ship to China.

Palestine had once been a possibility yet now they were headed in the opposite direction, about to sail into the unknown. Their journey was not the one they had imagined or planned but at least they were alive.

It appears my father was suffering from what today is recognized as post-traumatic stress disorder, in his case, the result of being overwhelmed by the stark contrast between normal life and the intense suffering in his recent past. This seriously debilitating condition can torment the sufferer indefinitely, as I understand it did my father, though I believe over time he made an admirable, though incomplete, recovery.

Noemi found an undated photo of my father with his head shaven, suggesting it was taken close to the time of his release from Buchenwald. Although the rim of his round-framed spectacles masks the light in his eyes, one can see enough to detect his hauntingly empty expression.

In this injured condition my mother took my father out of Europe forever.

What a voyage it must have been–my mother utterly drained by the agony of over three years of waiting and uncertainty. The last few months, in which she was trying to secure my father's release, must have tested every nerve in her body. And once she was reunited with her husband, a scene they'd anticipated over and over in their letters, reality prevented a retreat into romantic fantasies. He was not the healthy and amorous lover she had known before they were married and on her foreshortened honeymoon.

In the cramped quarters of their tiny floating hideaway, which doubled as my father's recovery ward, my mother was confronted daily with the evidence of their shattered dreams.

Therefore, more out of pity and staunch loyalty than the love that had flowed in their letters, my mother began the slow task of ministering to her sick husband. As patient and nurse, the couple, together with hundreds of other German and Austrian refugees, sailed to an unknown city more than eleven thousand kilometers away.

After a thirty-eight month separation, followed by a somewhat surrealistic month on the high seas, my parents arrived at their destination. Little wonder they never spoke about their journey and the faraway places like Aden, Suez and Singapore where the ship had docked along the way.

Trude, a refugee from Vienna who became a close family friend, met my parents soon after their arrival in Shanghai. She, her sister and brother-in-law, Meli and Stefan Koenig, had sailed to Shanghai on the same ship as my uncles, Heinz and Eric Meyer and Eric's wife Klara, some months previously. Trude described my father as being in the throes of a nervous breakdown, as it was referred to in those days.

"He was deeply depressed, locked inside himself. He didn't communicate at all and existed in a dream-like state."

I remember visiting Trude in Melbourne with my parents many years later. I was about ten at the time yet I can still hear the affection in her voice whenever she addressed my father, expressing the merest hint of wonder mingled with delight about the recovery of a now dear friend she had first met as a broken man.

My parents were met at the port by my mother's two brothers, Eric and Heinz, who had managed to flee to Shanghai soon after Kristallnacht since no visas were needed at either end at that time. Less fortunate refugees, with no family to greet them, were welcomed at the wharf by members of the local Jewish communities or by representatives of the United States Jewish Joint Distribution Committee who took them in open trucks to their temporary quarters.

I doubt my parents had ever given a thought to the existence of Jews in China before Shanghai became a place to which they could safely escape. Yet, the city had two well established Jewish communities; the affluent Sephardis had come from Iraq and created great wealth in the city in the mid-to-late nineteenth century, and the less affluent, but still well-to-do, White Russian community whose members had fled the Communist revolution in 1917.

Noemi believes that while my father was still recovering and unable to work, my parents, like so many of the refugees, were beneficiaries of one of the Jewish communities or "The Joint" as it was known.

My uncles took my parents to a large dormitory in the International Settlement, one of Shanghai's three foreign sectors, the other two being the French Concession and Hongkew (a separate area of the International Settlement),where they were assigned two beds.

The city, which had enjoyed economic growth since the 1850s, had turned into a huge hovel during the 1937 Sino-Japanese War. Hongkew or "Little Tokyo" as it was known to the Chinese, had suffered some of the heaviest fighting and left stretches of land in complete or partial ruin. It was inhabited mainly by lower-class Chinese laborers, the poorest Russians, Jews and some Japanese. Poverty, unemployment and what remained of cramped, sub-standard housing had resulted from hostilities which left the

Japanese in control of Shanghai. Apparently, even after much of it had been rebuilt, it could only be described as ugly and depressing. Just one street, Broadway, was lit up at night. Nevertheless, for about twenty-thousand German and Austrian refugees who were lucky enough to escape Europe before the outbreak of war, Hongkew was safe and satisfied two of their major needs: low rent and cheap food.

However, for about their first twelve months my parents were able to avoid the squalor of Hongkew, even though they'd had a taste of the appalling conditions in the dormitory where the overcrowding and lack of hygienic facilities would have turned my mother's stomach. Unfortunately, after just a few days there, they were obliged to leave because of my father's screaming nightmares which caused disturbances.

Since my parents were desperate to accommodate my father's problems, they finally found a room in the more expensive French Concession, a residential suburb with wide, tree-lined avenues by far the most beautiful of the foreign sectors in Shanghai. Probably they were helped to pay the rent by one of the Jewish Aid organizations. The suburb was mostly populated by wealthier Russians who had prospered during the previous twenty years and could afford the higher rents. There, my parents could manage my father's nightly horrors in private, and my mother could nurse her husband to better health away from the gaze of others.

My mother needed to work and anything she could earn would be a welcome supplement to their handouts. She found herself a job in a kindergarten (a job that Trude later took over) but soon had to pass it up because my father was still in need of constant attention during the day. Presumably, once he was settled for the night, she could think of evening work and fortuitously, found employment in a local bar. The job may not have appealed to her but she was in no position to be choosey. In any event, it was there she met the well-to-do Iraqi, Babel Jacobson (nom de plume) who offered my mother a position in his office. He also began an affair with her which I have written about in my memoir. My father, apparently, knew about the liaison but how it impacted my parents' marriage remains speculative. However, it is known that Babel arranged visas and paid for the sea voyage that saved the lives of my maternal grandparents. Thanks to Babel and my father (who later repaid him for the cost of my grandparents' tickets) they were able to leave Germany for Shanghai days before the outbreak of the war. Babel had also secured a visa for my grandfather, Karl Strauss, but tragically, as has already been mentioned, Karl became a prisoner of the Nazis and ended his days in Auschwitz.

Once my grandparents arrived in Shanghai there was a need for more living space. With two new additions to the family, my parents left their room in the French Concession and moved to a larger place in much poorer Hongkew where they remained for the duration of their stay in China.

By the time of Noemi's birth in July 1940, my father had recuperated sufficiently to be able to think once again of making a living.

Towards the middle of 1940, with money that seems to have been borrowed from his cousin Henry in the US, he accepted an offer to buy a Bill of Lading from someone who'd presumably paid a shipper for an order of expected goods. Exhibiting a trust that was unusual, given the betrayal and injustice he had suffered in Germany, he paid for the Bill without a guarantee that the seller was genuine, that the ordered goods were in good condition and that the shipment would actually arrive at its destination, given that the war was raging and uncertainties prevailed. While the gamble paid off it could as easily have been a disaster, another example of a potentially "wrong" decision. However, good luck seemed finally to smile on my father. The ship with its cargo arrived intact and, as Noemi says, "Dad made a packet," a small fortune, by hawking the goods around the city and selling them at considerable profit.

The windfall must have gone some way towards restoring his confidence and the family's belief in him. Capitalizing on his lucky break–and able to put to good use the English he had taught himself in prison–my father found himself an office in downtown Shanghai and began working as a merchant. He had now regained his drive to the point where our family could survive reasonably well, despite the impossibility of upgrading our housing since there were no better places to be found in the ruins of Hongkew.

However, all was not plain sailing. My father struggled with ongoing depression and fears that however much he earned there was never enough money. The legacy of the Nazis' confiscation of all his savings and his dread of inflation–which he'd experienced during and after World War I–left him with deep-seated insecurities about the state of his finances.

To add to his worries, my mother contracted Tuberculosis which seems to have been adversely affected by the inhospitable Shanghai climate. In a letter my father wrote to his cousin Hattie in the US he expressed his anxieties:

Shanghai 17th March 1941

The condition of my dear Irene here is nothing short of dangerous...her condition has not worsened but neither has it improved and it changes according to the weather...the doctor advises that curing her in the relatively near future would depend entirely on a change of climate and without such a change he can guarantee nothing...

The money I received from H last year has gone
into starting a business venture. I have not
been able to repay any of it due to continuous
bouts of illness. Besides, there have been not
inconsiderable expenses for the baby. But worst
of all is the unpredictable, erratic price rises
akin to inflation.

If I don't succeed in obtaining outside help I
will have to sell my business and stock. I am
uncertain how I will manage in such an event
though my main concern is Irene's health.

Though it is unknown whether "outside help" arrived, my
father's natural pessimism, his continuing unstable psychological
health and his panic over my mother's illness probably accounted
for his urgent letter to Hattie. Heroically, he kept working and
supporting the entire family.

As events transpired, my mother's lung condition improved
despite the suffocating summers and freezing cold winters.

At 81 Chusan Road, Hongkew our family lived in one very large
room on the second floor of a three-storey building. The space had
an enclosed veranda which served as my parents' bedroom, and
where I joined them in my cot in October 1944. The room also
served as a bedroom for my grandmother and sister, as a dining
room, and in one corner, concealed by a curtain, was a kitchen.
My grandfather, or Opa as we called him, slept in a bed under the
stairs.

Down a few steps from the main room, a bathroom with bath
and toilet was shared by all the occupants of the three-storey
house. Noemi recalls that our mother would not allow us to sit
down in a tub that so many other bodies used so we were washed
sitting on a small stool. The operation was quite involved since the

water had first to be boiled, though it was also possible to purchase it from hot water shops within walking distance of every home.

In her little makeshift galley, my grandmother prepared the family's meals on a spirit stove and baked cakes in a Dutch oven. She had received her training in the culinary arts at the Cordon Bleu Cooking Academy in Cologne, and in Hongkew demonstrated her talent for improvisation. My mother, it seems, left the cooking to her while she took care of the cleaning.

My grandmother also adopted the role of chief children's entertainer by staging puppet shows for us and our friends. Noemi says she stood on a chair behind her kitchen curtain and began each performance with the searching question to her rapt audience:

"Sind die Kinder alle braff? (Are you all being good children?), to which she received a resounding chorus of little voices echoing, "Jaaaa."

When she was not amusing the children, Oma, as she was known to everyone, spent her days behind the flimsy partition catering for seven adults who included my mother's two brothers and her eldest brother's wife, Klara, who often took their evening meal with us. Although Oma was used to catering for a family of five, her job was made more difficult because everything edible had to be boiled. The contaminated water and lack of refrigeration made eating fresh fruit and vegetables dangerous.

Another unpleasant feature of day-to-day life was the constant smell of kerosene. My mother once told me that the legs of all the beds had to stand in this petrol-derivative, to prevent crawling creatures from reaching the bedding. The combination of the intense heat, cooking odors and the smell of the anti-bug agent must have been suffocating.

Despite ever-present self-doubt and worry, my father's success as a merchant continued. My mother could even afford to give up a job in a flower shop and "play ladies," enjoying an easier life than she'd had in years. Noemi and I each had a European nanny to look after us while the family also employed a fellow German-Jewish refugee to do the laundry.

From all accounts, the Jewish refugees were a remarkable group who adapted themselves to their strange and difficult environment. David Kranzler, in his book, "Japanese, Nazis and Jews. The Jewish Refugee Community of Shanghai 1938-1945" (Yeshiva University Press, 1976) says they were able to transform a squalid and neglected Chinese suburb into the commercial hub of "little Vienna." Many of them, exceptionally enterprising, opened clothing shops, bakeries, delicatessens, coffee houses, restaurants and night clubs which gave the displaced foreigners a sense of home in the depressing ruins of Hongkew. They also managed to build a rich cultural life which included cinemas, libraries, theatres and recreational facilities despite the limited funds at their disposal. Kranzler describes Shanghai as a pulsating, cosmopolitan city where you could buy and sell almost anything for the right price. Other accounts refer to it as a cosmopolitan city which combined charm and elegance with corruption and crime.

The vibrant refugee community also set up radio stations which broadcast freely in a number of languages until the outbreak of World War II. Music on radio ranged from classical to jazz with one hour a week devoted to live performances by leading refugee musicians.

A flourishing German-Jewish language press produced three daily newspapers, two in the morning and another in the evening.

Noemi benefited from the refugees' initiative. Oma took her to see a Viennese pastiche operetta, Dass Drei Maedelhaus (House of the Three Girls) and she was able to take ballet lessons, and attend opera and concerts. At one such event she recalls the recital of a sentimental favorite of Jews around the world, "My Yiddishe

Mama," which produced weeping throughout the auditorium. Only about five years old at the time, Noemi remembers that everywhere she looked, people were crying. She didn't know, of course, that most of the refugees had left parents and other loved ones behind to an unknown fate in Europe.

Yet, despite their feelings of homesickness and dislocation the refugees created as normal a life as they were able in their depleted surroundings.

When Noemi turned six, my parents sent her to the Kadoorie School named after one of the Iraqi Jewish philanthropists who had made good in Shanghai in the mid-eighteen hundreds. The school was free for those youngsters who could not afford the tuition, and specialized in teaching English, a language Noemi didn't know. This did not stop my intrepid sister from speaking up when a young boy, trying to poke fun at her, called her a "blöde Gans" (silly goose). After the teacher intervened to ask what the boy had said, she stood up and proudly announced, "He said I am a bloody goose" an inspired guess in English at the German word "blöde," meaning "stupid."

My sister, much like my mother, has always been her own person. From early in her life, at times when Noemi experienced my mother's tendency to be impatient (a quality that never appeared in her letters to my father), my sister seems to have withstood it without it causing her much grief.

She remembers the day a huge fire broke out in the Hongkew fuel depot at the back of her school. In the chaos that ensued, Noemi adroitly made her way home while my mother, having heard of the explosion, frantically raced to the school to rescue her child. Unable to find her at the scene of the flames, my mother ran home only to discover Noemi, unharmed, who had come via a different route, excitedly telling Oma about the fire. Instead of clutching her daughter in her arms and praising her for her good sense, she showed her relief by growling at her. Far from being upset by my mother's reaction to stress, Noemi says she kept thinking how silly my mother was to react so angrily.

For several years the Jewish refugees experienced no negative interference from the occupying Japanese power, and were mostly left to their own devices. Yet the tolerance shown them was based on a stereotype of Jews as rich moguls who controlled world commerce and should therefore not be antagonized. At the same time the Japanese believed they could benefit economically from fostering cordial relations.

However, after the Japanese air force attacked the American fleet in Pearl Harbor in December 1941, and seemed to have scored a conclusive victory, conditions in Shanghai slowly began to change. Up until then, the refugees had enjoyed free access to radio and newspaper reports of the war in Europe. After Pearl Harbor, when America declared war on Nazi Germany and her Japanese allies, the refugees found their lives restricted and their information censored by their Japanese masters. Karl Bettelheim, whose parents had arrived in Shanghai from Austria in 1939, says:

"One day early in the war the Japanese soldiers came to our area and ordered all family members except my father out onto a nearby vacant lot where we were kept under guard, while a room-to-room search of all the dwellings in the area was undertaken. My father later told us that they carefully examined our radio to confirm that we could not hear foreign stations and then 'accidentally dropped it'."

For my father and, apparently, other refugees, the US entry into the war was a bright spot. My father had been waiting for that moment ever since Germany's invasion of Poland in September 1939, and even America's initial setback at Pearl Harbor did not cause him despair. He told Noemi he considered the first Japanese attack in the Pacific to be the beginning of the end. He believed that sooner or later US supremacy would win out because America was rich in raw materials and Japan was not. My father was right, of course, and six months after the sinking of the American fleet, the US Navy successfully retaliated by delivering their crippling blow to the Japanese at the famous Battle of Midway in June 1942.

Though this knock-out turned events around in the Pacific, it was another two years before the Americans and British landed on the French coast of Normandy in June 1944, and still another year before Nazi Germany was brought to its knees. In the meantime, my father and the other refugees had to survive the Japanese occupation.

While Japan's star was still in the ascendant early in 1942, rumors had begun spreading through the Shanghai community that the refugees would be forced into a ghetto in Hongkew. The Japanese never actually used the word "Jew" or "ghetto," preferring instead the terms "stateless refugees" and "designated area."

By the middle of that year the German refugees had to return their most recently acquired ID cards, known as Bridge Passes, for new ones called "resident certificates"[which] had an easily identifiable yellow stripe printed across the top…this act of being singled out again sent shudders of fear down the backs of many refugees.

Karl Bettelheim's family was no exception:

"I…remember my mother saying in an unguarded moment to a friend when she thought I could not hear her that she felt the Japanese might march us all out to a paddy field and shoot us…so such thoughts were certainly there."

From the time the rumors first spread about a ghetto, to the time the orders actually came, a whole year passed in which the Nazis had apparently been pressuring their Japanese allies to conform to the German model of anti-Semitism. Kranzler claims that "…in one fell swoop the refugees' fears of 'the long arm of the Gestapo' became a reality" when they were moved into the "designated area."

Our family, already residents of Hongkew, easily became part of the ghetto while those refugees who had established themselves in the French Concession were forced to dismantle successful businesses and start from scratch in far more crowded and poverty-stricken surroundings. Although it had no walls, refugees who needed to leave or re-enter the "designated area" were required to carry a pass with them at all times. Those, like my father, whose work took them out of Hongkew were known to the rest of the population by the red or blue metal badge worn on the lapel. Again, the Jews could not escape being forced to wear labels.

Trude, our family friend, remembers that obtaining a pass was often a nerve-wracking exercise. She says many in the Jewish community dreaded contact with the Japanese. She and other former Shanghailanders talk of a Japanese official named Ghoya who took a particular delight in pulling people waiting for passes out of long lines and taunting them, another echo of darker days. A short, irrational and unpredictable man, he called himself "King of the Jews." Historian Kranzler writes that one never knew when he would explode. He often arrived on the job with sweets for the children then a moment later would confiscate someone's pass, screech at the top of his voice until his face turned purple and then return the document to the hapless refugee as though nothing had happened. Karl Bettelheim's father was intimidated by Ghoya early on:

"My father initially had a pass to leave the ghetto for work, but soon afterwards gave it up because he could no longer face Ghoya's actions."

Before the ghetto became a reality, there was another move afoot which, apparently, not all the refugees were aware of and which mercifully did not eventuate.

In an interview with Fritz Kauffmann, former vice-president of the Jewish Affairs Bureau in Shanghai, conducted by Australian scholar and author Suzanne Rutland, Mr. Kauffmann spoke about a proposed Nazi plan in 1942 by young Japanese officers under Gestapo influence to exterminate the Jews of Shanghai. Fortuitously, the Jewish Affairs Bureau was notified by a sympathetic Japanese Vice-Consul, Shibata, whereupon Fritz Kauffmann attempted to take action. Immediately, however, he and other members of the JAB were incarcerated in the Bridgehouse prison and accused of spreading malicious rumors. His Japanese interrogators explained to him that, "the Japanese would never behave in such an abominable manner…because such a way of acting was against the Bushido philosophy."

Though the war in the Pacific continued, the refugees were not directly targeted. However, Trude remembers that a bomb meant for a Japanese radio station landed in the courtyard of the kindergarten where she worked. Dust and bricks fell into her niece's pram but luckily the infant was unhurt. Trude and the baby's father grabbed the stroller to move it out of harm's way but the shock of the explosion temporarily paralyzed them.

In the documentary "Shanghai Ghetto," by Dana Janklowicz and Amir Mann, one interviewer described the effect of low-flying planes emptying their consignment of bombs near the city: "You thought the world was coming to an end."

Others in the film talk of the unforgettable whistle of falling bombs and memories of shrapnel flying into their rooms.

Noemi recalls hearing the sirens blaring and says our family raced to the jail opposite our house to take shelter in its underground cells. Others, with nowhere to escape, hid themselves and their children under mattresses.

More than thirty people were killed during that raid and over two hundred injured. After the blast, the water and electricity were cut off for days, aggravating the already sub-standard living conditions.

When Germany finally surrendered on 8th May 1945, newsreels were screened in Shanghai showing the piles of starved corpses and half-dead walking skeletons the Allies discovered when they liberated the death camps of Nazi Europe. Trude says they were dumbfounded. Apparently it took some time to absorb what had happened and when the extent of the carnage sank in they were sick with grief. "We had no idea what the Nazis had done to the Jews but on the screen we saw the evidence of the terrible suffering."

Participants in the film, "Zuflucht in Shanghai, The Port of Last Resort," by Joan Grossman and Paul Rosdy, expressed similar reactions. Even those who had personally experienced anti-Semitism, had lived through Kristallnacht and knew about concentration camps were shocked beyond words when they understood their relatives had been murdered in death factories.

Soon the Red Cross posted lists of those who had survived the war and the camps and "The Port of Last Resort," shows the refugees milling around public notice boards straining to identify names of loved ones or anyone they may have known.

David Kranzler, who was also interviewed in "Shanghai Ghetto," confirmed that by and large the refugees did not know the extent of what had happened in Nazi Germany: when they understood the immensity of the tragedy and devastation caused by the Nazis they realized that despite the frightful hardships of daily life in the alien environment of Shanghai, "compared to their brothers in Europe they [had been] living in paradise."

This was probably the first time my father understood the truth about what had become of his father. Unfortunately, it is not known when, exactly, the two of them lost touch. In any event, what my father saw on the flickering black and white screen would have left him in little doubt. My mother, and grandparents, too, would have realized that members of their extended family had most likely perished. In this deplorable period of pain and sorrow the only comfort was the knowledge that the war in Europe had finally ended and now the time had come for the refugees to turn their thoughts to asylum in the West.

My father wasted no time in seeking ways to get our family out of Shanghai. Noemi says he foresaw the results of the fighting in the north between the Chinese Communists and the Nationalists that threatened to spread and engulf the Jewish refugees after the Japanese surrendered and withdrew. According to what my father told her in later years, he understood the totalitarian nature of Chinese Communism and knew the family had to leave as quickly as they could. For the second time in a decade, he applied to immigrate to the United States.

While my parents were waiting for our American papers, a cousin of my mother's in Melbourne, Berthold Meyer, who had come to Australia as a "Dunera boy" (a group of about two-thousand Jewish men who escaped the Nazis and sailed to Australia on the HMT Dunera), found our family's name on a Red Cross list of displaced persons and wrote to us with the good news that he'd be able to sponsor us. Suzanne Rutland writes that Australia's first Minister for Immigration, Arthur Calwell, who was sympathetic to Jews and their suffering in Europe, [had] announced "a migration program for survivors of the Holocaust on the basis of family sponsorship for humanitarian reasons." The cousin had lost his immediate family during the Holocaust and was eager to reunite with other close family members.

Glad of another iron in the fire, my father responded positively to the Australian invitation since waiting solely for US approval to immigrate was becoming too risky. As it happened, our Australian documents arrived first, together with the availability of a ship. My father grasped this tangible option despite the sad fact that it would separate him from his US cousins. A family friend told Noemi that my father was so desperate to leave that he bribed his Shanghai travel agent to get tickets for every member of our family on board the steamer "Hwa Lien," bound for the shores of the southern continent. What is notable about my father's decision is the speed with which he made it. He had clearly learned some tough lessons and had no second thoughts about what he needed to do.

With his good sense for business and a correct reading of the economic and political situation in China, he knew the time was running out in which he'd be able to take his hard-earned savings with him. His instincts were right. Just four months after our arrival in Australia new laws governing finance enforced by the Communists made it illegal to send money out of the country.

On 30th December 1946, my parents, my maternal grandparents and my sister and I boarded the "Hwa Lien" headed for Australia. It had taken eighteen months after the end of the war for our family to say farewell to Shanghai.

At the end of January 1947, after a miserable voyage on a rickety, barely seaworthy ship, our family arrived in Australia.

My father, who avidly followed world news, knew that in the country we were coming to Jews had risen to high public office and he therefore felt confident about bringing our family to Australia.

Lieutenant General John Monash, a Melbourne Jew of Polish origin and a brilliant tactician of the First World War had been knighted in 1918; Sir Isaac Isaacs, a Jewish judge, had been appointed Australia's ninth Governor General in 1930.

Two letters given to me by my father's cousin, Hattie, when I visited her in the US in November 2004, describe some of my parents' first impressions of Australia in the forties.

Hattie, who admitted she'd always had a soft spot for my father, was ninety at the time and partially blind. Yet she'd searched for the letters she received fifty-six years earlier ever since she heard I was coming. It was incredibly exciting "hearing" my parents express themselves in ways which needed little extrapolation. My father writes first:

Melbourne, 17th March 1947

We have been in Australia for six weeks now...we left [Shanghai] end of December and were at sea for four weeks. It was an awful journey on an old and too small boat although all turned out well.

My decision to leave Shanghai as quickly as possible turned out to be a correct one. Though I would probably have been in line to immigrate to America in March, leaving China would by now have been very complicated due to the foreign currency laws which were created in the interim...as it was, I was able to sell my wares at exactly the right moment, which, had I left it any later would have caused me to lose half my assets.

That circumstances in China were bound to go this way, I predicted a long time ago. The news from there speaks of social chaos and personal insecurity. When my friends asked me in puzzlement why I wasn't waiting to go to the US, I replied I was prepared to take the first boat out to wherever fate will take me, adding that from Australia I can always travel onwards.

Thus, we arrived here happily with my little parcel of six people and I must say we have come to a lovely country. The difference between Shanghai and here is so great that at first we thought we had arrived in paradise. Also, on our arrival we were lucky enough to find a three room flat with a large modern kitchen. The flat is situated in really beautiful surroundings directly by the sea, and when we go to the beach with the children, we only have to put on our bathing suits at home and "just around the corner" (written in English) we are already there. It really is a heaven for the children and I weep for the lost years in Shanghai.

The city itself is also very pretty and in no other place in the world have I seen such a lot of green parks...everything is very clean and naturally we Shanghailanders from the dirtiest city in the world look at everything through rose-colored glasses.

Two days later my mother wrote a separate letter in which a-typically she gives expression to her worries.

Melbourne, 19th March 1947

All my Dear Ones...we can happily confirm our great luck that we escaped the hell of Shanghai. Appalling news is coming from there and so we are terribly depressed that my two brothers, sister-in-law and their child had to stay behind. A dreadful epidemic of black plague has broken out once again and one of our good friends has come down with this illness. Many of our (prospective) immigrants have apparently already died. Though I was not very enthusiastic about our new race (the Australians) in the first weeks I am now pleased to be here despite the constant feeling of anti-Semitism. I suppose it will take time to get used to the place.

The contrast between here and Shanghai is so enormous I can't stop marveling at it. After eight years there we have totally forgotten how nice and clean things were in Europe…a friend here who has recently been on a world tour claims Australia is the most beautiful country in the world.

The children are crazy about the parks, the lawns and the beach and cannot get enough of them. Their greatest pleasure is to be allowed to romp around barefoot on the grass.

My dear mother…has made an excellent recovery…I myself have benefited from the clean air and can already notice a weight gain. After so many years we know how to appreciate fresh tomatoes and lettuce and the fruit that is available is a daily gift from heaven.

Life is very quiet here and one could almost believe Melbourne is a village. After 6:00pm one hardly sees people on the streets and in the beginning it was very lonely for us since we'd become used to the constant din in Shanghai…

Maybe we will still come to America. One of my mother's sisters also survived the Nazi era and is with my uncle in New

York...unfortunately, we could wait no longer in Shanghai in order to join you in America and I don't need to mention how much more we would have loved to be reunited with you all.

My parents' mention of the possibility of traveling on to America never materialized from which I assume they were relieved to be enjoying the normality and comfort of life in Australia. To the best of my knowledge they never again made any firm plans to uproot themselves.

I remember feeling sorry when I reached my teens and realized I'd grown up without knowing my first and second cousins. But how much more difficult had it been for my parents who had to wait another twenty years before they could comfortably afford to travel to the US to see loved ones from whom they'd been separated for so long.

Since my mother's two brothers and some close friends, the Koenigs, a family of five, were still stranded in "the dirtiest city in the world," my parents could not yet close the chapter on Shanghai. Or, perhaps I should say, it was my mother who could not close the chapter since it was she who was the family's "Good Samaritan."

My mother made it her business to apply for visas for her two brothers and the Koenigs. She wrote to the Minister of Immigration, Arthur Calwell, and caught a bus to Canberra, to speak with officials at the Department of Immigration. I can't imagine what her spoken English was like at the time but she was obviously undaunted by such minor details. After her dealings with the Gestapo she probably regarded the Australian bureaucrats as small fry. In any event, my mother's approach to the authorities proved successful, enabling her friends to secure entry permits and within about a year the Koenigs arrived. Perhaps the qualifications of the head of the household–Stefan Koenig had trained as a mechanical engineer–served as a positive indication to the government that the family would not become a drain on inadequate post-war resources.

Years later, when Stefan was seriously ill in hospital, my mother took up a collection from friends and acquaintances in order to help his family pay the medical bills.

My mother's older brother, Eric, fearing the Communists' advance on Shanghai, left for the US with his wife and young child early in 1948, when his US visa arrived before his Australian one. Her younger brother, my uncle Heinz, did not arrive in Australia until 1951.

Though I was only seven, I remember our family traveling to the airport in our new car to collect Heinz and my excitement at the prospect of meeting my uncle. I was too young to appreciate the meaning of the bitter-sweet reunion which, I assume, accentuated the absence of my other uncle who, had he come to Australia, too, would have completed my mother's immediate family.

As events transpired, my parents, the Koenigs and uncle Heinz had been lucky to make it to Australia when they did, before the initially favorable immigration policy became restrictive in the middle of 1947.

Suzanne Rutland describes the story of the hostile reaction to the Jewish refugees in the Australian parliament and press, emanating from a concern that the Shanghai Jews were corrupt undesirables who would take up already scarce housing intended for returning soldiers.

According to Rutland, the flames of this argument were fanned by one Major General O.C.W. Fuhrman, the Australian Consul-General in Shanghai, who tabled a secret report to the Australian Capital Territory, Canberra, in July 1947. The document stressed the unsuitable character of the Jewish refugees which negatively influenced the humanitarian policy of the Immigration Minister, Arthur Calwell. The Minister responded by imposing severe quotas on the numbers allowed to enter Australia, despite his great friendship with many Australian Jews and his admiration of the Jewish people.

Interestingly, my mother didn't need officialdom to tell her what she had picked up as an undercurrent of anti-Jewish sentiment in the general atmosphere.

Even after several years, I remember the caretaker of our flats calling my mother a "bloody Jew." What I don't recall is my mother's reply, or if, indeed, she replied at all. However, she was upset enough to tell my grandmother.

For the refugees stranded in Shanghai, Fuhrman's report to Canberra was a severe blow and resulted in only about two thousand and five hundred of nearly twenty thousand of them settling in Australia. Most of the remainder went to the US and Israel.

In any event, my parents' sheer relief at having arrived in safe, quiet, sleepy Australia of the 1940's, despite my mother's initial reservations, is evidenced in their two letters that Hattie had saved.

Recently, an article in _The Jerusalem Post_, hailed Melbourne, the city in which I lived for forty-four years, as the most livable in the world. In other studies that measure quality of life, Australia is consistently rated among the top ten countries.

My parents would have heartily agreed.

After twelve years of hardship and dislocation, they soon realized that Australia was their salvation, and Melbourne a welcoming city in which they could work towards establishing a comfortable life-style for themselves and our family. Throughout his life I remember my father expressing his heartfelt appreciation for his adopted country. Since I hadn't lived anywhere else at the time (I was an infant when we left Shanghai and later, in my mid-twenties, I lived in London for three years) I took our safe, easy and quiet lives for granted.

As we reached adulthood, my sister and I travelled the world. On her return to Australia, Noemi and her Greek husband George, settled in Melbourne, and raised their two children. Their daughter, Marina, in turn, chose to marry an American and live and raise their children in the US while returning often to Melbourne to see the family. Noemi and George's son, Philip, more firmly rooted in Australia, set his heart on going into politics, and at the age of thirty-nine became a Minister in the Victorian Government.

In his inaugural parliamentary speech, many years after they had passed away, Philip paid his deep respects to his immigrant grandparents referring to their trauma in Germany, their difficult years in Shanghai, their eventual arrival in Australia, and took the oath of office on his grandfather Gottfried's Bible. With the "miracle" of the Internet, I was able to watch his very moving speech in real time and knew how proud my parents would have been that their grandson, a first generation Australian, was enjoying professional success in the country they had been blessed to call home.

To my delight, and surprise, at the age of forty-seven I met my Israeli husband Ehud. I have now lived in Jerusalem for twenty-five years, but retain indelible links to Australia where my sister and her family live and where Ehud and I visit at least once a year.

Over the years I have made a good and happy life in Israel with new family and friends, but being Australian is a major part of who I am and will always hold an intimate, personal history known only to the family and close friends with whom I grew up.

It did not occur to me until I began writing my parents' story that fate had also taken them to a country at the other end of the globe from where they were born and raised.

As I pondered the meaning of this, I realized that our homeland continues to exist deep inside each of us, irrespective of where life leads.

I am certain that despite their enormous gratitude at being able to live a free and comfortable life in Australia, my parents always felt the gnawing loss of their homeland, the Germany that could have been.

END

9 781941 905142